OVERCOMING DEPRESSION

Dr. Henry W. Wright
MCM, DCTC

All Scripture quotations are taken from the King James Version of the Holy Bible.

Overcoming Depression
1st Edition

ISBN: 978-1-61184-123-7
Printed in the United States of America
©2017 by Be In Health®, Inc. All Rights Reserved.

Be in Health®

Dr. Henry W. Wright
4178 Crest Highway
Thomaston, GA 30286
www.beinhealth.com

If you wish to contact Dr. Henry W. Wright MCM, DCTC or Be In Health®, Inc. email info@beinhealth.com or call (706) 646-2074, toll-free (800) 453-5775, or fax (706) 646-2864

ISBN: 978-1-61184-123-7

No part of this book may be reproduced or transmitted in any form or by any means, electronic or mechanical- including photocopying, recording, or by any information storage and retrieval system- without permission in writing from the publisher. Please direct you inquiries to publishing@beinhealth.com.

Note: This book is not intended to provide medical advice or to take the place of medical advice and treatment from your personal physician. Neither the publisher, nor the author, nor the author's ministry take any responsibility for any possible consequences from any action taken by any person reading or following the information in this book. If readers are taking prescription medications, they should consult with their physicians and not take themselves off prescribed medicines without the proper supervision of a physician. Always consult your physician or other qualified health care professional before undertaking any change in your physical regimen, whether fasting, diet, medications, or exercise.

DISCLAIMER

Be In Health®, Inc. does not seek to be in conflict with any medical or psychiatric practices nor do we seek to be in conflict with any church and its religious doctrines, beliefs, or practices. We are not a part of medicine or psychology, yet we work to make them more effective, rather than working against them. We believe many human problems are fundamentally spiritual with associated physiological and psychological manifestations. This information is intended for your general knowledge only. Information is presented only to give insight into disease, its problems, and its possible solutions in the area of disease eradication and/or prevention. It is not a substitute for medical advice or treatment for specific medical conditions or disorders. You should seek prompt medical care for any specific health issues. Treatment modalities around your specific health issues are between you and your physician.

As individuals in this organization, we are not responsible for a person's disease, nor are we responsible for their healing. All we can do is share what we see about a problem. We are not professionals, we are not healers, we are only administering the Scriptures and what they say about this subject, along with what the medical and scientific communities have also observed in line with this insight. There is no guarantee that any person will be healed or any disease be prevented. The fruits of this teaching will come forth out of the relationship between the person and God based on these insights given and applied. This organization is patterned after the following scriptures: 2 Corinthians 5:18-20; 1 Corinthians 12; Ephesians 4; Mark 16:15-20; 2 Timothy 2:24-26.

PREFACE

I ask for much grace and mercy in the reading of this book because this teaching is not designed to be a theological dissertation but designed to be an insight into a problem and its solution: Overcoming Depression. I reserve the right to revise this information as God increases the depth of my understanding.

I don't want this book to become a method or a science or a formula or a quick-fix to take the place of relationship with God. The theme in this book is the consequences of rejection that cause separation from God, His Word, His love; separation from ourselves; and separation from others.

One of the things that concerns me for those that will use this book to try and help others is that they will make it into a science or, at worst, use the knowledge in a legalistic manner to condemn others. A heart of compassion is the key to using this book.

The Authorized King James Version of the Bible is the foundation for this teaching. Please do not change the King James Version as a scriptural foundation as this teaching will lose the integrity and intent of its meaning.

This book is taken from a transcription of a live seminar on the subject of Overcoming Depression. There will be some repetition of material, as I frequently review a prior session at the beginning of a new one. Some of those redundancies have been left in this document, as it was felt that they added to the overall understanding of the teaching that was given. My teaching style also includes repetition because of Isaiah 28:9-13.

> [9] **Whom shall he teach knowledge? and whom shall he make to understand doctrine?** *them that are* **weaned from the milk,** *and* **drawn from the breasts.** [10] **For precept** *must be* **upon precept, precept upon precept; line upon line, line upon line; here a little,** *and* **there a little:** [11] **For with stammering lips and another tongue will he speak to this people.** [12] **To**

whom he said, This *is* the rest *wherewith* ye may cause the weary to rest; and this is the refreshing: yet they would not hear. [13] But the word of the LORD was unto them precept upon precept, precept upon precept; line upon line, line upon line; here a little, *and* there a little; that they might go, and fall backward, and be broken, and snared, and taken.

Isaiah 28:9-13

Here are some tools to help you as the reader maximize the use of this book:

1. For convenience to the reader, the scriptures are quoted in their entirety whenever they are referenced in the main text. These scriptures are **bolded** in the text.

2. The content of this material is broken down into chapters and sections within the chapters. The chapters isolate specific subjects and build toward a conclusion. The sections represent smaller specific aspects of the general themes.

Table of Contents

Chapter 1
Understanding the Foundation for Depression 1

Section 1: Our Spirituality Impacts Our Physiology 7

Section 2: Depression is A Curse 14

Chapter 2
Depression Impacts Your Spirit, Soul and Body 21

Section 1: Taking Ownership of Your Life 28

Section 2: Spirit-Soul-Body Connection 36

Chapter 3
Our Relationships and Depression 45

Section 1: Insights into Specific Conditions 50

Section 2: True Diseases Versus 'Sin-Dromes' 63

CHAPTER 4
CHOOSING TO OVERCOME DEPRESSION   73

Section 1: God's Code for Life   80

Section 2: A Different Way of Thinking   92

CHAPTER 5
'GOS-PILLS' FOR YOUR LIFE   99

Section 1: Your Journey with the Word   105

Section 2: Renewing Your Life Like the Eagles   114

Section 3: Concluding Prayer   117

CHAPTER 1:
UNDERSTANDING THE FOUNDATION FOR DEPRESSION

Does the Bible say, "the Joy of the Lord is somebody else's strength?" No. It says, "The Joy of the Lord is my strength!"

Then he said unto them, Go your way, eat the fat, and drink the sweet, and send portions unto them for whom nothing is prepared: for *this* day *is* holy unto our Lord: neither be ye sorry; for the joy of the LORD is your strength.
Nehemiah 8:10

When you make decisions you are taking ownership of something. In the day that you take ownership of something, it's either for good or not so good. You have to decide you are going to take ownership of your life. It is your life. You cannot blame God. You cannot even blame the devil. And you cannot blame your friends. You may say, "Well, if there weren't a devil, then I wouldn't have a problem." Yes, you would. You still have to deal with your decisions and issues arising from being trained by sin. I am not trying to condemn you, but I need you to think about your life. I am going to approach this subject thoroughly, trying to keep it as non-clinical as possible to give you an insight into the inner-workings of the various types of depression. The problem we have, even in the church today, dealing with different forms of depression is that we somehow forget that we are a triune being. By triune being, I mean that we have three components to our make up. We have a spirit, we have a soul (our mind), and we live in a body.

And the very God of peace sanctify you wholly; and *I pray God* your whole spirit and soul and body be preserved blameless unto the coming of our Lord Jesus Christ.
1 Thessalonians 5:23

Chapter 1

Everything is inner-healing. Everything is soul management. We are attempting to deal with thoughts and traumatic experiences without understanding the source of those thoughts and the spiritual battle waged. The course of action we take is to use what I call 'chemicals' to manage our imbalances without even considering what is causing the imbalance. These 'chemicals' are pharmaceutical drugs meant to make us feel better for the moment. So we end up in a drugged state temporarily to keep us from hurting ourselves and hurting others. That is not how it should go.

Now the world is filled with hopelessness, anger and despair. No question about it. Often times we feel we have no hope. If you are born again, you are sons and daughters of the living Father. You should have a good day. Why not? Your Father is God. I mean, what is wrong with that? You have a birthright, and you have a future that even transcends death that the world does not have.

> **[9] And they sung a new song, saying, Thou art worthy to take the book, and to open the seals thereof: for thou wast slain, and hast redeemed us to God by thy blood out of every kindred, and tongue, and people, and nation; [10] And hast made us unto our God kings and priests: and we shall reign on the earth.** Revelation 5:9-10

I would like to take you on a journey. At some point, I will talk about who you are as a triune being: you are a spirit, you have a soul, and you live in a mobile home (physical body). You are not the mobile home. You live inside the mobile home. Your spirit man is who you are on the inside. Your body is the outward vehicle by which you express yourself and live.

Sometimes I, with tongue and cheek, will joke and pick with the medical community and the psychiatric community in my presentation. If you are a doctor reading this, please realize that I am trying to make a point in this discussion. I am not trying to be disrespectful to your industry. I pick and have a little fun with the medical community, because they are not treating you as a triune being. They are treating you as a being that has a soul just like other animals. They are actually treating us like an animal. They think we are an animal because in their schools of learning and through zoology and the rest of the study of anatomy and physiology, they have come to the conclusion that is all we are. The other day, while talking to someone,

UNDERSTANDING THE FOUNDATION OF DEPRESSION

I said, "It might be better if you went to a veterinarian than to your local doctor. At least they will pat you on the head, scratch you behind the ear, and, occasionally, give you a pat on the butt and say, 'Good boy.'" That is very therapeutic. Come on now. If somebody would just scratch you behind the ear, pat you on the head, and on the butt, you would be happy. Of course, I am joking. However, the reality of going to a doctor is not that comforting. They inform you of how awful you are doing and how they can help make you feel 'awful better.' I suspect you know this is the truth. You know this is the truth from your experiences.

I have a doctorate in Christian therapeutic counseling. All that means is that I understand you from the inside out. Knowing you from the inside out means that I figure out what causes your problems physically, psychologically and spiritually. So I am not going to approach depression from managing your physiology through drugs, therapy, guided imagery or through whatever popular modality that they are trying to do to keep you from floating out of your chair to keep you earth-bound a little longer. No, we are not going to go there.

At the same time, I think we need to deal with some clinical terms from the standpoint of education. I would like to take the time to do so. Depression involves being depressed. Is that surprising? What is depressed is your lack of elevated mood. So things are down. Your chemicals are down, and you have fallen off your chair because if you are a believer the Word says, "You have been seated in Heavenly places with Christ Jesus, far above all principalities and powers."

And hath raised *us* up together, and made *us* sit together in heavenly *places* in Christ Jesus: Ephesians 2:6

In depression, you have fallen off your Heavenly seat, down to the beggarly elements of the world and you end up swimming around in that mess. Then you think the mess is part of who you are. I have a few phrases I tell people that have diseases. I say, "You may have a disease, but you are not a disease. When God created you, He did not say, 'There is my beloved, diseased son and daughter in whom I am well pleased.'"

Chapter 1

> And lo a voice from heaven, saying, This is my beloved Son, in whom I am well pleased.
>
> Matthew 3:17

Something has joined us that is not of God. Would you agree with that? You may have depression, but you are not depression. If I can remove the disease and I can remove the mood swings and depression, guess who I have left? You without the problem. That is the gospel. But the gospel does not just involve healing. Everybody wants some anointed person to come and zap them. By 'zap' them I mean that people want to be prayed for and immediately become well. Essentially, they want to be 'zapped' back to health. That is what they are looking for, some 'anointed zapper.' Many of you have been zapped by anointed people, and you are still the same as before you got zapped. Then they do not know what to do with you. They just keep zapping you in Jesus' name, hoping it sticks one day. Not realizing that the problems we have are the byproduct of a journey—spirit, soul and body.

Is depression a state of being or is it actually a 'being' that is in the state of existence? The person in that state of being can have an aversion to activity, an aversion to being around people, and they can go into isolation and withdraw. Withdrawal is one of the worst ways depression can hurt you. One of the first steps to healing from depression is to come out of isolation. Plan to be around people you do not like. That will challenge you. If you choose to confront and survive this step you will be better for it, but we usually do not deal with life. We withdraw.

Depression involves your thoughts, your behavior, your feelings, and your sense of well-being. People with a depressed mood can feel sad. They can feel anxious. They can feel empty. They can feel hopeless, helpless, worthless, guilty, irritable, ashamed, or restless. They may even lose interest in activities that were once pleasurable to them. They may experience overeating or loss of appetite, have problems concentrating, remembering details, or making decisions. They may even contemplate, attempt, or commit suicide. They may develop insomnia, excessive sleeping, fatigue, aches, pains, digestive problems or reduced energy.[1] Yuck. I do not feel good thinking about the consequences. Those problems can be severe.

---

1. American Psychiatric Association (2013), Diagnostic and Statistical Manual of Mental Disorders (5th ed.), Arlington: American Psychiatric Publishing, pp. 160–161, ISBN 978-0-89042-555-8, retrieved 1 MAY 2017

UNDERSTANDING THE FOUNDATION OF DEPRESSION

Now, there may be a depressed mood. Let me say this to you, it is probably normal to experience bouts of sadness or loss because of life circumstances. But usually, we recover because 'the joy of the Lord is our strength.'

Then he said unto them, Go your way, eat the fat, and drink the sweet, and send portions unto them for whom nothing is prepared: for *this* day *is* holy unto our Lord: neither be ye sorry; for the joy of the LORD is your strength. Nehemiah 8:10

We live by godly principles which defeat the things that are not of God. As a result, we usually come out of it. As we move through this teaching, we will explore a subject that is not well understood. We do not understand the subject of temptation. We do not recognize the source of temptation. God does not tempt you. You may have an original thought from your own mind that is ungodly, and that is certainly possible. However, we do not know nor are we readily taught in the Christian church that we can be tempted by an invisible kingdom that answers to Satan. It is very clear in Ephesians that your battle is not with flesh or blood.

For we wrestle not against flesh and blood, but against principalities, against powers, against the rulers of the darkness of this world, against spiritual wickedness in high places. Ephesians 6:12

What does that mean? It means that your battle is not even with yourself ,because you are also flesh and blood. Surprise, surprise. Why would you become your own enemy? Be kind to yourself. Your battle is not even with yourself, and your battle is not with others. They may manifest stuff that makes you feel sad or rejected or abandoned or whatever the case may be. Your battle is not with them, but your battle is with principalities and powers. Your warfare is with principalities and powers, and spiritual wickedness in high places and the darkness of this world. That is your battle. It is with invisible beings.

In this teaching, I am going to explain how invisible beings speak to you and by which channel. They give you thoughts and feelings as if it were your own mind. Church, you are so easily influenced by that other kingdom. That other kingdom

Chapter 1

provides you with a thought. You take ownership and you allow these beings to manifest through you. That is how it happens. That is how you have been had. You are not rejecting evil thoughts, or taking ownership for listening to them by doing an inventory of your soul, personality, and spirituality. Because you have had a thought does not mean you have to take ownership of it. You do not have to believe every thought that comes to your mind is yours.

There is not one person on this planet that is immune to temptation. There is not one person that is immune to feelings of hopelessness, despair, fear, anxiety, bitterness, and rejection. There is not one person that does not experience those thoughts traveling through your consciousness either by actual thoughts or by feelings, emotions, and impressions. Not one person. Every day these ideas are like ticker tape on Fifth Avenue streaming through your mind. Now you do not have to tune into it. You do not have to take ownership of these thoughts.

One of my new phrases about dealing with temptation and things that are not of God is—flush it. I am not trying to be disrespectful and gross, but I have reasoned with people about temptation by using this bathroom metaphor. I have said, "You know, when you drop some logs in the toilet, you do not invite your friends over to come look at the architectural structure or to enjoy the aroma. You do not call your friends and say, 'You gotta see this stuff in the toilet, it came out of me'. Maybe they would say, 'It's about time.'"

Then why do we embrace thoughts that are just as disgusting and just as non-essential? God created you to "flush" things that are not good for you. Why don't we learn to flush our souls and our spirits, not just our bodies? Come on now and think this through. I am giving you a parable. All the religious spirits are upset now. They may be saying, "I don't think a man of the cloth should talk this way." I am not a man of the cloth. I am your brother. Are you tracking with me? Maybe that is how you defeat depression, 'flush it.'

Quit taking ownership of things that are not of God. You may say, "Yeah, but..." That is the response of a spiritual 'goat.' Goats have excuses for why they cannot obey the Word of God. That is not the reaction of sheep. Sheep never say, "Yeah, but..." They reply, "Aaa-men. Aaa-men." Goats reply, "Yeeah, but..."

And before him shall be gathered all nations: and he shall separate them one from another, as a shepherd divideth *his* sheep from the goats: Matthew 25:32

Understanding the Foundation of Depression

Regardless of what you say to a goat, you always have a rebuttal. No matter what you say or how positive you choose to be, you have spiritual sass as a response. The reason you have this sass is that the person does not want to change and follow God.

Section 1
Our Spirituality Impacts Our Physiology

'Depressed mood is a feature of some psychiatric syndromes; such as major depressive disorders.'[2] This information is clinical stuff; this is man's understanding of what is happening to you. They have you stereotyped and categorized. They will quickly find you in the DSM5 (Diagnostic and Statistical Manual of Mental Disorders) and tell you all about your problems. I can go to the DSM5 Manual and there you are. However, that is not who you are. The description found in there is what you should not be. It is easy to classify people in their hopelessness and despair, but not many individuals in the industry of psychiatry and medicine know how to prevent it. This teaching is instructing you in how to prevent it. I am going to tell you how to understand it and prevent it. If it is already part of your life, I will tell you how to be released from it. Freedom is your birthright.

There are typical reactions in life to such things as experiencing loss and bereavement that involves mourning and sadness. However, when you are stuck in depression, you can be prescribed antidepressants and all sorts of drugs that are given to manage your biochemistry imbalance. Every drug you take has a side-effect. Certain antidepressants produce depression. Certain antidepressants given to children increase suicidal ideation. Do you know the side effect of a drug can result in another problem? Do you know the side effect of a drug can be another disease or disorder? Then you may take another drug to balance the side-effect of the initial drug. When you do this, you are involved in polypharmacy because the new drug is attempting to balance the side effects of the first drug. Yet that new drug may have side effects of its own. All of a sudden, you are a chemical experiment, and your body has gone wacko. This is not God's will. It is not what He created. When God created Adam and Eve, He did not say it was good. He said, "It was very good."

---

2. Diagnostic and Statistical Manual of Mental Disorders, Fifth Edition (DSM-5). American Psychiatric Association. 2013

CHAPTER 1

And God saw every thing that he had made, and, behold, *it was* very good. And the evening and the morning were the sixth day.

Genesis 1:31

So, what happened to very good? We are going unfold what happened to very good as we move through this teaching.

Let me skip through some of these clinical terms. There are things that happen in life and childhood. There is neglect. There is unequal parental treatment of siblings. That favoritism creates rejection. There is physical abuse, verbal abuse, and there is sexual abuse. There are life circumstances that we encounter that affect us and make us feel awful feelings.[3] A feeling may not be real. A feeling may just be temptation from that other kingdom. Remember to trust God instead. 'If God be for you, who can be against you?'

What shall we then say to these things? If God *be* for us, who *can be* against us?

Romans 8:31

'If God be for you, who can be against you?' Who cares if somebody else does not like you? They do not like God then, because He made you. If they do not like you, they do not like God. So why would you want to hang out with people that do not like God? He is the author of life. He is the author of sanity. He is the author of health and life and everything that is good. That is what you were given at the cross unless you want to go back and live the old life. I thought it was called a 'new life.' Then why do we bring the 'old life' with us? It is because we are comfortable with the failures of the past. Yes, we are comfortable with it. We have something to talk about. We want people to come in and look at our stuff. That way, in our self-pity, we can bring them down to our level of depression by commiserating over the failure of our lives. We are trying to get a few people to agree with us that we are worthless. Even if they do not agree with us, we might respond, "Tell me about it. Well, this is just the way I feel."

---

3. Christine Heim; D. Jeffrey Newport; Tanja Mletzko; Andrew H. Miller; Charles B. Nemeroff (July 2008). "The link between childhood trauma and depression: Insights from HPA axis studies in humans". Psychoneuroendocrinology. 33 (6): 693–710. doi:10.1016/j.psyneuen.2008.03.008. PMID 18602762. Retrieved 24 April 2017

Understanding the Foundation of Depression

If it is true that we should only go by our feelings, Then the Scripture should say, "For as many as are led by their feelings are the sons and daughters of God." Now, what does that Scripture really say? "For as many that are led by the Spirit of God, they are the sons (and daughters) of God."

For as many as are led by the Spirit of God, they are the sons of God. Romans 8:14

If you are going to be ruled by your feelings, you are not working with the Spirit of God. Now it is okay to have feelings that are productive and positive. That is part of your soul expression. According to the Word of God, being happy is normal and being unhappy is abnormal. Having hopelessness and despair is abnormal. Having hope is normal. Having fear is abnormal and having faith is normal. When did we decide to stay abnormal? I thought the cross made it possible that we could be changed to be normal.

I am asking you to take ownership of your life. If not, then you are choosing to live in fear. Being afraid that only adversity will come to pass in your life requires no faith. To take ownership of your life, you are going to have to mix your faith with the Word of God that speaks about who you are and who God is. Why would you die because of the sins of another against you? Why are you taking all of the sins of other goofy people into your body and believing their lies against you? What God said is true. You may respond, "But I've sinned, I have problems, I'm not perfect." So what? There is none righteous. Welcome to the crew. Let me repeat for emphasis. There is none righteous. Welcome to the body of Christ! But if we confess our goofiness, He is faithful and just to forgive us and to cleanse us.

If we confess our sins, he is faithful and just to forgive us *our* sins, and to cleanse us from all unrighteousness. 1 John 1:9

However, often we do not even take the time to repent, because we love self-pity more than faith. Self-pity is the super glue of hell that binds you to the past. This is your life. You have the Spirit of God in you, get up and let God and you get on with it.

Chapter 1

Yes, but you may have the temptation to say, "Yeah, but, but, but…" Here we go again—goats. You are acting like the goats of His pasture. 'Yeah, but you just don't understand.' Tell Jesus about that. He died for your sins. He was beaten, brutally scourged, bloodied, and he was forgiving those that just did it.

There are things in life that cause distress. The Bible says, "Many are the afflictions of the righteous, but the Lord delivers them out of them all."

Many *are* the afflictions of the righteous: but the LORD delivereth him out of them all.

Psalm 34:19

The Bible says, "When this horrible thing has come upon you…" You may say, "Oh, why me? Oh, my God, I'm the worst. I'm a worm. I'm slime." However, the Bible says, "When this horrible fiery trial comes upon you, don't think that it's just special to you, but these things are common to man."

There hath no temptation taken you but such as is common to man: but God *is* faithful, who will not suffer you to be tempted above that ye are able; but will with the temptation also make a way to escape, that ye may be able to bear *it*. 1 Corinthians 10:13

[11] If any man speak, let *him speak* as the oracles of God; if any man minister, *let him do it* as of the ability which God giveth: that God in all things may be glorified through Jesus Christ, to whom be praise and dominion for ever and ever. Amen. [12] Beloved, think it not strange concerning the fiery trial which is to try you, as though some strange thing happened unto you: [13] But rejoice, inasmuch as ye are partakers of Christ's sufferings; that, when his glory shall be revealed, ye may be glad also with exceeding joy. 1 Peter 4:11-13

"Oh, it's just me, I'm the only one that God doesn't love." If you entertain those thoughts, you are listening to the devil. God loves you. He proved it at the cross. Would you say amen to that?

I am sharing information with you that God can use to help you prevent depression, if you have it get free of it, and then also make you expert at helping others. The information I am giving to you is for you to use in your personal life

Understanding the Foundation of Depression

and with your friends, your families, and strangers. Knowledge can help you to help them understand this incredibly dangerous pathway of thought and how it comes. Then you can help others. Would that not be good? Then you do not have to send them to me or someone else. You can help them. I do not want to be worn out trying to help everyone by myself. I want you to be equipped to help others as well. You will be able to assist them. It would be great if we could help others together.

There are many psychiatric syndromes. We are addressing some of worst issues because of their impact on so many lives. The first area is bipolar, also known as manic depression. Everybody wants to know about manic depression/bipolar. I will examine the various aspects of bipolar and its implications for our spirituality and psychology. There are some gender differences related to bipolar. Women have a higher rate of depression than men, but the incidence of suicide is greater in men than in women.

As we look into the genetics of inherited bipolar, females have a greater incidence than males. One of the reasons for that is interesting, biologically, because it is a defect inherited on the X chromosome. Females have two X chromosomes; males only have one. So the biological incidence and probability are increased in females than in males if it is genetically inherited. Most professionals whose studies and case histories I have tracked feel that for the most part, bipolar is genetically inherited.

Every one of you has at least one X chromosome. Do you see it inside of your body? Maybe not, but it is in there. In some cases of manic depressive illness, it is X-linked. This gene is inherited through the mother. The reasons will be explained in greater depth later, but it is important to address the question—why the mother? When someone comes around that has been diagnosed with bipolar/manic depression, I look to see if their mother has it or their grandmother because it is very common. It is familial. Track the word down: familial. That would be characteristic to certain families.

I am going to get into familial spirits a little later to show you how Satan's kingdom is tracking your family tree and why. That other kingdom is here to give thoughts to your family tree. As far as I am concerned, usually if there is bipolar or manic depression inherited in the family tree, then the thoughts have already been

Chapter 1

in action causing problems. These thoughts are an indication to me of the failure of men to be proper husbands and fathers in the generations as far back as you can look. The father establishes the safety and the emotional well-being of the family, not the mother. Now, mom can be great, but there has to be a male present that establishes a safe place. Without that safe place, everyone is scattered in their thinking. Everybody needs a safe place.

It is amazing in creation how children begin their life in this world. When a child is born they begin the journey of awakening to these strange people (i.e. their parents) that have sounds coming out of their mouths. They begin to understand that certain sounds are associated with an item or person. That is how they learn language. A classic example of the desire God put in the hearts of humans is the first person children identify through speech. The first word that most children male or female say, in the learning curve of speech, is "Dada," for Dad. Is that not true? Because God has birthed within them, in their creation, something looking for a father. That earthly father is to represent God the Father of love from Heaven.

In this scenario, mom is okay with it for a while, because the child is talking and saying something. At the same time, she is feeling rejected because she wants to hear 'Momma.' So, she says, "Okay, Johnny, that's Dada. Cool, you got it! Now, let's hear 'Momma.'" And Johnny says, "Dada." "No, no, no, no it's not Dada, I'm 'Momma.'" He replies, "Dada."

While I am playing with this concept and having a little fun with you, it is important to understand that from a young age, we have a need for a father. If this flow of safety from the male is broken, there is no covering. The husband should be the head of the household providing protection and direction for the home.

But I would have you know, that the head of every man is Christ; and the head of the woman *is* the man; and the head of Christ *is* God. 1 Corinthians 11:3

If a man does not provide covering, he is repeating Adam's problem today. It is the same thing that came in through Adam when he refused to cover his wife, Eve. He did not reason with her to refuse the temptation to eat the fruit. In fact, he blamed her that he listened to her and ate the fruit. 'It's that woman you gave me,

UNDERSTANDING THE FOUNDATION OF DEPRESSION

Lord. I would have been a spiritual man and obeyed, but it's because of her.'

And the man said, The woman whom thou gavest *to be* with me, she gave me of the tree, and I did eat. Genesis 3:12

Many men will not be correct spiritually and they blame it on their wives. As a result, she is oppressed and suppressed believing she is the source of his problems. This creates all kinds of spiritual problems in the flow of the generations. Blessings are not coming to that household, because blessings only belong to those who are doers of the Word. You can read that for yourself in Deuteronomy 28:1-2. 'And it shall come to pass if you hear what God said and you'll do it then all (I like the word 'all') these blessings shall come upon you and overtake you.'

[1] And it shall come to pass, if thou shalt hearken diligently unto the voice of the LORD thy God, to observe *and* to do all his commandments which I command thee this day, that the LORD thy God will set thee on high above all nations of the earth: [2] And all these blessings shall come on thee, and overtake thee, if thou shalt hearken unto the voice of the LORD thy God. Deuteronomy 28:1-2

Everybody today is into the 'prophetic.' They have a need to know if someone has a 'word' about future blessings and outcomes for their life. Instead of giving you a new 'word,' I am going to give you a prophetic statement, but it is not coming from me. It is coming from the Word of God. Deuteronomy 28:1 says, "And it shall come to pass." Is that prophetic? It is as prophetic as it comes. You do not need another word from the Lord; it is already there in the Word. 'And it shall come to pass if...' So does the word 'if' make the prophetic conditional? Yes. No one wants to make the prophetic conditional, but God's Word requires obedience. God is true, but not all men and women want to be true to God's words. He will never change. He says, "I change not." We want to change the Word of God because it requires that we change into His image. However, if you are going to defeat depression and prevent it you have to prepare to be changed into His image through obedience to His Word. The Bible says, "From glory to glory we are being changed (present progressive tense)

13

Chapter 1

into His image." The words 'are being' connote continually being changed into God's image as a process not as a single, solitary event.

> **But we all, with open face beholding as in a glass the glory of the Lord, are changed into the same image from glory to glory, *even* as by the Spirit of the Lord.** 2 Corinthians 3:18

God is not depressed. God has no fear. God has no bitterness. God has no hopelessness. God has none of the things that we struggle with and if we have been made in His image, what in the world did we lose? His image! You became born again by the Spirit of God so you could begin the journey of being changed into His image, not so you could continue to act like you did before you were saved. But you have to take ownership. 'And it shall come to pass if the man or woman will hear what God says and do it'; there is action. Not just knowledge, but action—being a doer, not just a hearer. You will never defeat the enemy or depression if you do not take ownership of your life. It is your life. It is your responsibility to take ownership of it. Quit blaming others because you are not happy.

Father God is happy. You are His sons and daughters. Why are you not happy? Being a son and daughter of God the Father, you should be ecstatic! Every day you should be ecstatic with joy and happiness that you have made peace with the Father of all spirits. You should be ecstatic! Yes, you are sons and daughters of God. Yes, I am Henry, son of God. Somebody might say, "Yeah, well you're the son of the devil." To that, I would respond, "No, you believe that because you have an awful accusing spirit. You did not save me, He did. God saved me. He didn't need your permission to save me. Father God didn't need your permission to release the Holy Spirit to me. He didn't need your permission, He just decided. If He decided, I say amen to Him." I say amen to 'the Amen'" who said it to Himself when he said amen. Amen? So be it.

Section 2
Depression is a Curse

Prophetically, it says there in Deuteronomy 28:16 "And it should come to pass if…"

UNDERSTANDING THE FOUNDATION OF DEPRESSION

15 But it shall come to pass, if thou wilt not hearken unto the voice of the LORD thy God, to observe to do all his commandments and his statutes which I command thee this day; that all these curses shall come upon thee, and overtake thee: 16 Cursed *shalt* **thou** *be* **in the city, and cursed** *shalt* **thou** *be* **in the field.** Deuteronomy 28:15-16

'If' means there is a condition. If you hear what God says, but you will not do what He said, then all these 'junky yucky' awful things shall come upon you and overtake you. In this Scripture is all manner of biological disease. Within that are all kinds of psychiatric disease. You can find losing your farm to foreclosure; somebody else reaping your crop instead of you. There is losing your wife to another man and losing your business to bankruptcy. Even hemorrhoids are in there. Right in there are hemorrhoids.

The LORD will smite thee with the botch of Egypt, and with the emerods, and with the scab, and with the itch, whereof thou canst not be healed. Deuteronomy 28:27

In my experience, people tend to squirm when curses are brought up. Often I will refer to them as 'blanks' instead. So are hemorrhoids a blessing or a 'blank'? If you think hemorrhoids are a blessing, I need to talk to you. I guess it all depends on where you are sitting. If you think that hemorrhoids are a blessing, why do you go to the doctor trying to get rid of them? It would be as if someone said, "Thank God for my hemorrhoids. They are a blessing." That is crazy. You are trying to authenticate something that is not of God. Wow. What else can I tell you if that is what you choose to believe?

Here are some additional facts for you. What is depression? Is it an illness? Now, I want to reveal something to you. Depression is not an illness. It is not a disease. It is a syndrome. There is nothing biologically wrong with the human brain. If there were something wrong with the human brain, it would be organic damage maybe from an injury or from a birth defect or something of that nature. But when you start taking medicines or antidepressants, there is not one part of your body healed. There is nothing wrong with your body.

Behind depression are issues related to neurotransmitter imbalances and chemical imbalances including norepinephrine and serotonin and dopamine.

Chapter 1

Some thoughts can cause biochemical imbalances. The term 'hypo' indicates under secretion of various neurotransmitters, and 'hyper' is the overproduction of various neurotransmitters.

We are going to inspect some case histories from my experiences of healing. People have been healed of depression related issues. As we take a look at what is causing specific diseases such as Paranoid Schizophrenia and even right down to Parkinson's disease, we will see they are not true diseases. What is the difference between what we are covering in this teaching and when you go to the doctor? They are going to give you a diagnosis. But what is the point? The diagnosis gives you an indication there is something wrong. However, it is more important to understand what is malfunctioning in the body and why. I am not against a diagnosis; I am against not dealing with the etiology. The word etiology means to cause or causative. What causes this process and what causes the body to go into an imbalance of homeostasis? In other words, what is causing the body to become imbalanced? What causes the interference of nerve signals? What causes hormones to be over-released or under-released? What causes neurotransmitters to be over secreted or under secreted? What is the causative action? Rather than give a drug to balance out the imbalance where is the sanity that says we need to stop what is causing the imbalance thereby eliminating the need for the drug in the first place? Did you get that? Let me repeat it because it is worth considering. Rather than giving a drug to try to balance the imbalance, with all of its side effects, we need to dig a little deeper and find out what is causing the imbalance. If we are no longer imbalanced, there will be no need for the drug to balance the imbalance with all the side-effects. What I offer you is no drugs at all. I offer you the truth. You do not need a bunch of pills. You need one pill—the Gos-'pill.' That is all you need, and there are no side-effects. But you have to take ownership of truth and work with it and live it, and you have to have your minds changed, and your spirit man changed. You are going to have to change your entire personality to be like Him. Why not be like your Father? Father God knows everything. I want to be like Dad. I had an earthly dad I did not want to emulate. It was not always pleasant. I am a preacher's kid, and there were problems in our relationship.

Depression involves a mixture of the body responding to mood, thoughts, and

UNDERSTANDING THE FOUNDATION OF DEPRESSION

emotions. Any time you do not deal with thoughts that are negative that are making you feel awful, it eventually will become part of your persona. What is a persona? Your personality. Satan and his kingdom know how to train you in mood disorders. He knows how to entrap you with his personality. You are so easily deceived. Your enemy and his kingdom do not even have to work up a sweat to defeat you. The harsh reality is that we do not know our enemy. In fact, they figure you are already defeated, because you are ignorant. Of what? Satan's devices. But you are told in the Word of God not to be ignorant of Satan's devices and his methods and his mythologies.

Lest Satan should get an advantage of us: for we are not ignorant of his devices.
2 Corinthians 2:11

People do not know what to do when prayer does not work. For many, prayer and laying on of hands is all high vector and hype; slap you with oil, knock you over and hope you get up well. If you are not healed after being prayed for you are told you just need more faith. No, you might need sanctification, not more faith. You can use all the faith you want. You can hype yourself up. You can quote the Word. You can jumpstart it, but if you have something in your life that is empowering the enemy to afflict you, your faith will not work until you deal with the issue that gave the devil ownership of that part of your life. Then your faith will work in defeating him. I implore you to get out of this superstitious church mentality. The church is writhing in superstition and the vanity of improper conclusion.

I conduct conferences across North America. During some of these conferences, I conducted a survey of diseases in Christianity in various cities. Maybe some of your have been to those conferences. I put a table out, and I would put pieces of paper listing diseases from A-Z; 'A' like alopecia, allergies or angina to 'Z' for 'zebra-titis.' I like to joke about 'zebra-titis.' It is my humor, and at a conference, two people wrote that they struggled with zebra-titis. I guess it could be a form of OCD. People could struggle over whether a zebra is white with black stripes or black with white stripes. Granted this was hypothetical, but we have various struggles. Incredible.

In my journey, I found the average audience I have addressed in the past is sick.

Chapter 1

They are sick Christians. At conferences, I successfully predicted the number of those sick with diverse diseases and I was never wrong one time. I can go to your church in your city, walk in on a Sunday morning and I can tell the pastor what is in that audience and who is there and what they have, and their hands will go up. That pastor has a sick church. But, bless God, we believe we are dying to go to heaven in our diseases. We do not realize there is another way out.

The average audience that I have addressed has over 300 to 400 different diseases and over 2,000 total, because some individuals have more than one disorder or disease. That is in every audience I have ever addressed. I am sure some of you reading this, also, struggle with these issues. This should not be. Healing is supposed to be the children's bread. What happened to the children's bread? We are not eating bread that is why. We are not eating the manna of God's Word. We are eating that other stuff. Ideas based upon men's minds; fear based, ignorance based. They call it 'practicing medicine' because doctors are still practicing. What they call healthcare is in fact, disease management. They bewitch you with the term healthcare, when in fact, all you are doing is being managed in your disorders. 'He who the Son sets free is free indeed.' I repeat, "He who the Son sets free is free indeed."

> **If the Son therefore shall make you free, ye shall be free indeed.** John 8:36

Classical depression can be described as a dysthymic disorder which includes all the clinical symptoms. Persistent sad, anxious or empty mood.[4] It might sound like whimpering and whining. 'Nobody knows the trouble I've seen, but my Jesus. He still loves me doesn't he?' I have taken a different perspective. I am a dead man, and dead men are just happy to be alive. Once I was dead in my trespasses and sins, then my Father in Jesus name sent the Holy Spirit to get me to make me a son. I am a dead man, and this dead man is happy every single day. You do not have to jumpstart me. I am alive on the inside all the time, because dead men are just happy to be alive. It is not a matter of being dead, but realizing that we can be dead to or let go of our past and the patterns of behavior and thought that held us down.

---

4. Gabbard, Glen O. Treatment of Psychiatric Disorders. 2 (3rd ed.). Washington, DC: American Psychiatric Publishing. p. 1296

Understanding the Foundation of Depression

> I am crucified with Christ: nevertheless I live; yet not I, but Christ liveth in me: and the life which I now live in the flesh I live by the faith of the Son of God, who loved me, and gave himself for me.
>
> Galatians 2:20

Maybe you have not died to something to become alive. Perhaps you are hanging onto death and thinking that you should be living. You cannot live and hold on to the attributes of what produces death. We need to deal with the spiritual first, psychological, and then biological. We need to deal with feelings of hopelessness or pessimism—there is no faith there. We need to address feelings of guilt, worthlessness or helplessness, loss of interest, decreased energy. I thought it was significant that there is no single known cause of depression. In the upcoming chapters, I am going to cover four areas that depression can come.

Sometimes depression or feelings of depression can be caused by what you eat producing a chemical imbalance in your body. A basic definition of depression is that it is the result of a chemical imbalance in the body. That is one of the main definitions of depression. The result of a chemical imbalance in the body.

As an interesting side note, once in a while, someone comes to me with a low-grade depression. They are not quite on top of their game. They feel a little down. The first thing I ask them is, "Are you on artificial sweeteners?" Many people are on artificial sweeteners, because of fear. Now there are diabetics that cannot take in sugar, and that is not the situation we are addressing. Most people that are on artificial sweeteners, do not have diabetes. Their avoidance of sugar is fear based, because they do not want to gain weight. Studies have suggested that artificial sweeteners may contribute to weight gain.[5] Additionally, another study suggests that certain types of artificial sweeteners are possibly heightening the severity of feelings of depression in those with a history of depression.[6] We have been had.

---

5. Yang, Qing. "Gain Weight by 'going Diet?'" Artificial Sweeteners and the Neurobiology of Sugar Cravings: Neuroscience 2010." The Yale Journal of Biology and Medicine. YJBM, June 2010. Web. 24 Apr. 2017

6. Walton, R. G., R. Hudak, and R. J. Green-Waite. "Adverse Reactions to Aspartame: Double-blind Challenge in Patients from a Vulnerable Population." Biological Psychiatry. U.S. National Library of Medicine, July 1993. Web. 24 Apr. 2017

Chapter 1

The villain is laughing his head off at our fear based thinking. So when dealing with people on artificial sweeteners, I say, "Do me a favor. Come off artificial sweeteners for thirty days because it's going to take thirty days for your bodies to re-acclimate to your biochemistry. It's not going to happen overnight."

CHAPTER 2:
DEPRESSION IMPACTS YOUR SPIRIT, SOUL AND BODY

I do not want to appear insensitive to the depths of where depression can take a person. Do not think that I am flippant about the condition. But part of compassion is helping you to defeat it and prevent it. So there have to be tools for overcoming depression. I know when a person is in depression the last thing they want to hear is something positive, because they may think you are being insensitive. It is not insensitive to be positive. As a preface, I am not insinuating that defeating depression is 'mind over matter.' When I say take ownership of your life that is not mind over matter. There is a battle for you–period. Every day there is a kingdom assigned to interfere with your journey of sanity, peace, and health. What should you do? Embrace the concept and plan of being an overcomer. You need to plan on being an overcomer. 'There is a narrow gate that leads to life. Few there be that find it.' That narrow gate is not out here somewhere that you have to chase down. The narrow gate is right in the midst of the wide gate.

> **[13]Enter ye in at the strait gate: for wide *is* the gate, and broad *is* the way, that leadeth to destruction, and many there be which go in thereat: [14]Because strait *is* the gate, and narrow *is* the way, which leadeth unto life, and few there be that find it.** 2 Matthew 7:13-14

There are many voices in the wide gate asking you to deviate from the principles that will take you into eternal life. I want you to enjoy the future Jesus described. Jesus said, "If you'll overcome as I overcame, as I have sat down with my Father, you too shall sit down with me and my Father." I want that for all of you. 'To he that overcomes shall inherit all things.'

Chapter 2

He that overcometh shall inherit all things; and I will be his God, and he shall be my son.

Revelation 21:7

Somebody said, "Well, this is so hard." Can I give you a reality check? I do not mean to be harsh in framing the next statement. I care about what you are going through, and I do not want this phrase to come off wrong. However, we need to reason together about life events. In the greater scheme of things, I do not care what you are going through. Ultimately, I do not care what you are currently going through nor anything you are going to go through tomorrow or will ever go through here on this planet. We need to be 'spiritually minded' rather than 'carnally minded' living only for the current moment. I want to give you a prophetic statement to change your perspective. A hundred years from now your current situation will be the last thing on your mind. So stop making it so eternal now. I hope that will help you. There is hope for your future.

A *Psychology Today* article says, "There's no single cause for depression, rather it is likely the result of a combination of factors."[7] I want you to track with me. One of these factors is genetic. Earlier I mentioned the genetic connection to cases of bipolar. In medical science, they see evidence of a genetic linkage in this form of depression. In some cases, it can be linked to a recessive gene through the mother. Our genes also indicate that we could be carriers of many other problems as well. However, God did not create these genetic defects. God did not create mankind with these issues. There are thousands of different genetically inherited diseases and disorders. Through biology and science, humans have identified countless genetically inherited maladies. God did not create mankind defective. God did not create man diseased or insane, but something joined mankind that made him diseased and allowed him to have some 'bats in his belfry tower.' This caused confusion and double-mindedness and all these feeling that come.

On the subject of the soul, I have some really interesting data concerning dementia and Alzheimer's disease. Recently, I have been doing some research into

---

7. "Depressive Disorders." Psychology Today. Sussex Publishers, 27 Dec. 2015. Web. 24 Apr. 2017

why dementia is increasing at 400% in the next 20 years.[8] I have had some sneaking suspicions about neurological degeneration. My research concerns the causes of neurological degeneration; some of the reasons are spiritual and some are chemical. There is some strong evidence that artificial sweeteners are producing neurological degeneration and that could be the reason why we have neurological pathways that are damaged producing some forms of dementia.[9]

Alzheimer's is a different story. It is an autoimmune disorder. The previously mentioned form of dementia is not. They do not know what causes it, but somehow the pathways of memory are not working. In the case of Alzheimer's, the immune system is producing peptides or a plaque that builds up on the neurological memory pathways of recall. A person with Alzheimer's has not lost their memory. It is still there, but the thought cannot get through because it bumps into these plaques or peptides that are formed by the immune system. Therefore, the person cannot have the cognition or remembrance.

As a side note, the other cause of dementia I brought up is quite serious, so I challenge you in your thinking. Artificial sweeteners can potentially cause trouble as I mentioned earlier. I suggest you do research for yourself and make your decision as to whether it is wise to use them or not. There are a lot of natural alternatives to artificial sweeteners. I would certainly change my lifestyle to save my mind. A word to the wise right now, folks. We have had to make some changes in our lives to deal with a world that is insane.

From various chemicals in food products to pharmaceutical drugs, we must be thoughtful about what we put in our bodies. With the highest level of psychiatric problems, the United States of America is number one in the world with 11.5% of its people on some form of psychiatric medicine.[10] America, these are serious times.

---

8. Brookmeyer, R., and S. Gray. "Methods for Projecting the Incidence and Prevalence of Chronic Diseases in Aging Populations: Application to Alzheimer's Disease." Statistics in Medicine. U.S. National Library of Medicine, n.d. Web. 24 Apr. 2017

9. I. Ashok, Dapkupar Wankhar, Wankupar Wankhar, and R. Sheeladevi. "Neurobehavioral Changes and Activation of Neurodegenerative Apoptosis on Long-term Consumption of Aspartame in the Rat Brain." Journal of Nutrition & Intermediary Metabolism 2.3-4 (2015): 76-85. Web. 24 Apr. 2017

10. Moore, AB Thomas J. "Demographic Differences in Adult Use of Psychiatric Drugs." JAMA Internal Medicine. American Medical Association, 01 Feb. 2017. Web. 24 Apr. 2017

Chapter 2

This teaching is probably prophetic for you. It is meant to help you to awaken, so you do not have to be a victim of ignorance any longer. You may say, "Well, I don't like that term. I don't like the word ignorance." Well, the Bible uses that word, and it says that God's people are full of ignorance. The Bible says, "There is a way that seems right unto a man, but the end thereof is destruction (or death)."

> **There is a way which seemeth right unto a man, but the end thereof *are* the ways of death.** Proverbs 14:12

If you are following an instinct, it may not be based upon knowledge or wisdom. Right now, America is filled with superstition and living by instinct and beliefs based upon past wrong conclusions. The newer theories are not any better. America is no longer a Christian nation, folks. Pray for revival in America. We need God to be our solution. This teaching is meant to give you insights into physiological and psychological problems as well as how to return to Father God to be healed.

Besides environmental issues, psychological factors can cause depression. The medical community uses the term 'psychological factors,' but neglects a vital part of the solution. Nowhere in psychology including Christian psychiatry, the older DSM4 manual, or the new DSM5 is the realm of the human spirit ever considered a factor in the healing and prevention of depression. It is all 'psyche.' It is all soul. You might not need more counseling. Instead, you may need to get rid of a devil that is talking to you. This might sound very direct, but you need to tell it to 'shut up.' You have to decide you are not going to be influenced by it anymore. These evil spirits need to be cast out of you so they are in torment and you are at peace. When it is cast out to a dry place, it is tormented because it does not have you to bug. On the other hand, you are at peace because you are listening to God and not the evil spirit's insane ideas. So tell it to go to its dry place so that you can think straight.

> **When the unclean spirit is gone out of a man, he walketh through dry places, seeking rest, and findeth none.** Matthew 12:43

But the church is not being taught you have an enemy. Many churches seldom, if ever, talk about Satan and his kingdom. The new 'grace mistake' teachings say

DEPRESSION IMPACTS YOUR SPIRIT, SOUL AND BODY

you do not have an enemy. You can live like 'hell' and sin without considering the consequences. Because you are loved you are going to heaven. Grace covers you and protects you regardless of your decision to rebel against God's Word. They teach there are no repercussions for practicing sin. Some churches even teach that repentance is irrelevant to your everyday journey of overcoming as a believer. The church is sick, and no one dare say it is. I say, "It is sick." It is not God's will that it be sick. We ought to be the light of the world.

> [13] Ye are the salt of the earth: but if the salt have lost his savour, wherewith shall it be salted? it is thenceforth good for nothing, but to be cast out, and to be trodden under foot of men. [14] Ye are the light of the world. A city that is set on an hill cannot be hid. [15] Neither do men light a candle, and put it under a bushel, but on a candlestick; and it giveth light unto all that are in the house.
>
> Matthew 5:13-15

You ought to be the shining light of God's mercy, and His greatness, and His power, and His health, and His sanity. You should not represent the opposite. It may seem like I am preaching, but this is a vital part of solving problems that seem clinical and intellectual. Your spirituality impacts your health in every other dimension.

In depression, parts of the brain responsible for regulating mood, thinking, sleep, appetite and behavior can be affected. Additionally, important neurotransmitters, chemicals the brain cells use to communicate, appear to be out of balance. Some types of depression seem to run in families suggesting a genetic link. However, depression can occur in people without family histories as well. You can do extensive research on this subject if you want to be a clinician and have all the facts, but you will not find any lasting solutions. The only solutions they have are antidepressants and other treatments.

Depression may also be a consequence and side effect of other medications. One resource I found indicates: "Certain medications used for depression as well as some medical conditions such as viral infections or a thyroid disorder can cause the same symptoms as depression."[11] So you need to be careful that depression is not a side effect of another biological disease. If a physical cause for depression is ruled

---

11. "Diagnostic Evaluation and Treatment." Northwest Behavioral Medicine. N.p., n.d. Web. 24 Apr. 2017

Chapter 2

out a psychological evaluation that includes a mental status exam should be done.

If there is no biological origin, then a condition is considered psychological. Antidepressants work to try and normalize naturally occurring brain chemicals called neurotransmitters, notably serotonin and norepinephrine. Other antidepressants work on the neurotransmitter dopamine. These three major neurotransmitters are problematic in most psychiatric disorders. All the enemy has to do is manipulate your biochemistry. He does it through the influence of thought. You are so easily controlled by the enemy. His kingdom gives you a thought, lets you believe it is you and then convinces you to take ownership. Your body will conform to your thoughts. 'So as a man thinks in his heart so is he.'

> **For as he thinketh in his heart, so *is* he: Eat and drink, saith he to thee; but his heart *is* not with thee.** Proverbs 23:7

Then you have serotonin re-uptake inhibitors or SSRIs including Prozac. People take Prozac because they are in a state of depression. I want to focus on the subject of how Prozac works. Prozac does not increase serotonin. Serotonin release can only be increased by a person feeling good about themselves—period. The pharmacological action of Prozac prevents normal functions of serotonin recirculating through the body. The inhibitor chemically blocks or shuts down the return ports for serotonin that are floating in the synapse at the end of the dendrites to keep it from going back in and being recirculated. Because there is not enough serotonin when a person is depressed the pharmacist has learned that he can give a drug, such as Prozac, that will cause the return ports to close thus leaving more serotonin in circulation trying to give the increase of a 'feel good.' However, serotonin levels have not been increased whatsoever.

How does someone end up on Prozac? Hypothetically, there may be a guy that does not feel good about himself. He is not on top of his game. Nobody loves him. So he goes to the doctor, and he has a low-grade depression and feels 'blah,' melancholy, blasé, and the doctor says, "Oh, I have something for you. I'll give you some Prozac. That will pick you up." Prozac is widely available. At its core, Prozac changes the way your body functions to bring you a measure of peace and soundness. When it is

Depression Impacts Your Spirit, Soul and Body

first introduced into the body, it takes time to alter the biochemistry of the body to produce changes. These changes create a need for the drug to maintain a desired level of peace. So this man will begin to take Prozac, and for the first 90 days it is going to condition his body to receive more.

However, Prozac has some serious side effects. For this man, it will potentially produce problems once it is introduced into the chemistry of his body. The first side effect of Prozac is that it may cause an anxiety disorder. Before he was dealing with feelings of depression, but now he is anxious and looking around wondering what could go wrong. As a result of that side effect, he may have to take an anti-anxiety drug to balance out the anxiety triggered by the Prozac. This problem could become paranoia. Is that a worthwhile permanent solution?

There are about two dozen major side effects of Prozac. The next major side effect of Prozac is the loss of libido or sex drive. [12] This guy is not feeling good about himself, he has an anxiety disorder as a side effect, and now he has lost all interest in his wife. You think he had problems to begin with? Wives expect to be pursued properly by their husbands. Wives need to expect to be pursued because that is their faith and hope. Men need to 'step to the plate' and satisfy that God-given requirement by making their wives feel valued. If a man loses all interest in his wife, he is about to live on the roof alone by himself. There is not going to be peace in that home.

The next major side effect of Prozac is psychosis. You can do your own research if you like. There have been scientific studies that have suggested a possible connection between increased violence and use of SSRIs. [13] Another major side effect of Prozac is anti-social behavior. I think God had something different in mind to help us with our battle with ourselves about ourselves. You are required to accept yourself by God. Why? Because He has accepted you. Who is greater? You or God? God is greater than you, and He has accepted you through His Son. If you, who are lesser than God, do not accept yourself you overthrow God's covering in your life.

---

12. Clark MS, Jansen K, Bresnahan M (November 2013). "Clinical inquiry: How do antidepressants affect sexual function?". J Fam Pract. 62 (11): 660–1. PMID 24288712

13. Molero, Yasmina, Paul Lichtenstein, Johan Zetterqvist, Clara Hellner Gumpert, and Seena Fazel. "Selective Serotonin Reuptake Inhibitors and Violent Crime: A Cohort Study." PLOS Medicine. Public Library of Science, 15 Sept. 2015. Web. 24 Apr. 2017

Chapter 2

> **God forbid: yea, let God be true, but every man a liar; as it is written, That thou mightest be justified in thy sayings, and mightest overcome when thou art judged.** Romans 3:4

> **I will praise thee; for I am fearfully *and* wonderfully made: marvellous *are* thy works; and *that* my soul knoweth right well.** Psalm 139:14

Actually, you enter into something called self-idolatry. You have made an idol of yourself, because you have chosen your thoughts over what God has told you in His Word. You are telling God that you do not care what He says. You are no good. Everybody knows it. He made a mistake in saving you. You are a worm, and you are no good. You are calling God a liar. I am not interested in calling God a liar because He is truth. You cannot call truth a liar. You call a lie a lie. 'God is not a man that He should lie nor a son of man that He should lie.'

> **God *is* not a man, that he should lie; neither the son of man, that he should repent: hath he said, and shall he not do *it*? or hath he spoken, and shall he not make it good?** Numbers 23:19

God is truth. He is sanity. God has no depression. God has no anxiety. With God's way and solution, there is no side effect. Other side effects of antidepressants can be mild and annoying. These may include: dry mouth, constipation, bladder problems, sexual problems, blurred vision, dizziness, drowsiness. That is not good. The most common side effects of SSRIs are headaches, nausea, nervousness, and insomnia, agitation, feeling jittery, and sexual problems.

Section 1
Taking Ownership of Your Life

How do you begin to deal with depression? Take ownership of your life. How do you move forward if you have been ensnared? You may have had a thought, "Well, I want to go from black to white. I want this problem gone—immediately." You may not come out of depression rapidly just because of this teaching. You may not come out of depression because you declare, "I have enough faith to defeat it." That is

Depression Impacts Your Spirit, Soul and Body

because your mind has been trained to think in a way that produces depression. Your persona or your personality may have been shaped by the training of evil spirits. Those thoughts are no longer just temptation anymore. Those thoughts are not just an enemy trying to influence you. Those thoughts become a part of your biology. You can be rewired to think like evil spirits. Then it becomes a part of who you are. Your enemy knows exactly how to train you in the law of sin. Exactly.

You need tools to help recover yourself from depression and to prevent it. Beginning to understand information about short term memory and long term memory are vital tools. Another related part of this conversation is understanding who you are created to be by God.

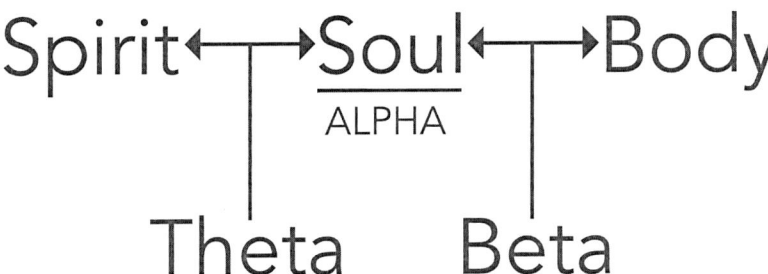

Diagram 1: Spirit, soul and body are connected by three brainwaves. Theta connects the spirit and soul. Alpha is contained to the soul/mind and Beta helps us process our external world and situations.

You are a spirit. You have a soul. And you live in a body. The soul is the bridge between the physical world and the spirit world. Psychiatrists do not acknowledge you are a spirit being. If you saw me teaching right now, it would be stored in short term memory. You would perceive me through your five physical senses. Two of them in particular; sight and sound. The images that you are taking in today are being recorded at the soul level in your cerebral cortex because of beta brainwave activity. Without this brainwave, you would not hear me or see me. You would be a vegetable. In that situation, you might be able to smell, taste, and touch. However, it would be difficult to speak to you through touch, taste, and smell. You have probably heard of the mind-body connection, many people have heard of it. But few people are teaching the spirit-soul-body connection. Understanding the spirit dimension of who we are is a vital missing piece to overcoming depression.

In the absence of considering our spirituality, we rely entirely on scientific research which results in being stuck with some improper conclusions. I have no

Chapter 2

problem with humans looking at what God has created. I am indebted to science for making accurate observations of external phenomena. I am not against science. Science is the evidence of what God created, and I am happy to continue learning. So I am not an enemy of science, but I am an enemy of incomplete hypotheses and wrong conclusions. I am an enemy of superstition and anyone that does not validate the reality of the spiritual dimension; including God and who we are as spirit beings. Denying the reality of the spirit world is a form of tunnel vision and ignorance at the highest level.

You perceive the world around you through beta brainwaves. You are recording what you see and hear at the cerebral cortex. Right now, as you look around, it is recorded in short term memory. Changes take place as you begin to consider or continue to think about something. As I understand it, learning and retention of information require you to have heard something or seen something in its entirety six times just to retain 25% of what was seen or heard. We are all a little slow, are we not? It takes time for us to process and remember information. Now when the enemy comes along, he does not give you a thought just six times. He may give you those thoughts every day for 365 days a year, because he wants to program you to have a depressive disorder. You are in his sight, because of lack of understanding of his plans and schemes. You are ignorant of Satan's devices because you may have only considered what you perceive in the physical dimension. Science has not told you about your enemy. The fallacy of science is it only believes what it can see. That is why many in science hate the Bible because it asks them to consider things they cannot see. They cannot quantify and qualify the spiritual dimension and they go 'tilt' and reject it. You are told not to judge things just by what you see. Jesus said he did not judge things just by what he saw, because the Spirit of God was working with him to discern things well beyond the physical dimension.

> **15 Ye judge after the flesh; I judge no man. 16 And yet if I judge, my judgment is true: for I am not alone, but I and the Father that sent me.** John 8:15-16

He even knew the thoughts of people's hearts. He understood their 'invisible' thoughts. It was part of his faculty and discernment as a work of the Holy Spirit. If

Depression Impacts Your Spirit, Soul and Body

you begin to think and meditate on things over and over again, there is a biological phenomenon that happens. It is called protein synthesis. It involves an element of DNA and RNA, specifically RNA. If you begin to think over what you have seen or heard repetitiously, that thought, which was short term memory, through the process of protein synthesis becomes permanently part of your biology. That sinful thought has become flesh to your flesh. It has become part of the way you think.

But you are to allow the Word of God to become 'flesh of your flesh.' You are to meditate on the Word of God. How often are we suppose to meditate on the Word of God? Day and night.

This book of the law shall not depart out of thy mouth; but thou shalt meditate therein day and night, that thou mayest observe to do according to all that is written therein: for then thou shalt make thy way prosperous, and then thou shalt have good success.

Joshua 1:8

God knows that if you begin to meditate on His Word day and night that it will become permanently part of your biology. Now you have an antidote to the law of sin. If you do not have an antidote to the law of sin, all you have is the law of sin and no other thoughts to counteract and defeat it. You can go on an antidepressant, but it does not help you change your mindset. In fact, an antidepressant will keep you from dealing with the issues of your life. You will have a measure of relief without dealing with the underlying spiritual root cause. That is why I said, "Coming out of these personality profiles is not easy, because you have to retrain your minds." As you read and apply God's Word, which is life and truth, you begin the process of coming out of depression. This process is the opposite of being programmed by the law of sin attempting to influence and tempt you.

And be not conformed to this world: but be ye transformed by the renewing of your mind, that ye may prove what *is* that good, and acceptable, and perfect, will of God. Romans 12:2

[25] **Husbands, love your wives, even as Christ also loved the church, and gave himself for it;** [26] **That he might sanctify and cleanse it with the washing of water by the word,** [27] **That**

Chapter 2

he might present it to himself a glorious church, not having spot, or wrinkle, or any such thing; but that it should be holy and without blemish. Ephesians 5:25-27

In Romans 7, Paul said, "In my members, I have two laws…I have the law of God, and I have the law of sin."

²² For I delight in the law of God after the inward man: ²³ But I see another law in my members, warring against the law of my mind, and bringing me into captivity to the law of sin which is in my members. Romans 7:22-23

That applies to us as well. 'I have the law of God, and I have the law of sin' and so do you. You can still remember how to hold a grudge and become bitter. But the Word of God says, "You are to forgive your brother." How often? One time? Seven times? No. Jesus said, "Seventy times seven (70x7)."

Jesus saith unto him, I say not unto thee, Until seven times: but, Until seventy times seven. Matthew 18:22

Even though we know that we are to forgive our brother seventy times seven, the law of sin is so strong in our members we go into unforgiveness, bitterness, and repaying evil with evil. All of the sudden we are establishing that other kingdom and the Spirit of God is not there to protect us. God does not honor the law of sin. He only honors the law of God. If you do not have the law of God, you do not have a chance. You could be a Christian and go to church, but without God's Word, you are 'easy pickings' for the enemy, because you have nothing to compare to your thoughts. When thoughts come to you, you cannot determine if they are of God without knowing His Word. It must be compared to what you have read in God's Word, and if it contradicts the Bible, you must be willing to cast it down and discard those thoughts.

I want to leave you with an impartation not just the facts. I could give you so many facts that you would fall asleep. But what good is it to give you facts if you do not know what to do with them? I can break down all the DSM5 definitions of melancholy and bipolar and unipolar and all the rest of these conditions. I could go

DEPRESSION IMPACTS YOUR SPIRIT, SOUL AND BODY

into all the clinical definitions and you might nod off as you read. With knowledge about a disease, you still might not know how you got stuck with it and how to defeat it. I would be derelict in my calling if I did not show you how to prevent it and how to be free of it. I am not selling any medications today. I have no special therapies to offer you. You do not need 30 years of counseling. You need revelation from the truth. A lot of people are making money off your inability to take ownership of your life. A lot of people love to manage you in your problems; it is good business. At least you have somebody to dump on in disease management; it is therapeutic to a certain extent. The Bible says, "Confess your faults one to another," but then it says, "that you may be healed."

> **Confess *your* faults one to another, and pray one for another, that ye may be healed. The effectual fervent prayer of a righteous man availeth much.** James 5:16

What good is it to confess your faults one to another and never be healed? There is a place of confession one to another. There is a place to bear each other's burden, and I thank God for those that are laying their lives down to help people think straight. But, I have to tell you something. I have been unable to help one human in 30 years of ministry that would not take ownership of their life. Why? Because they have no faith. And it says, "Without faith, it is impossible to please God."

> **But without faith *it is* impossible to please *him*: for he that cometh to God must believe that he is, and *that* he is a rewarder of them that diligently seek him.** Hebrews 11:6

God will not force us to listen to Him and agree with Him. I imagine God saying, "Well, I cannot help you either. You are down there 'mully grubbing,' feeling down, and bad about yourself. You're having breakfast, lunch, and dinner with the enemy." After visiting the doctor to find out what is wrong, you receive a diagnosis of depression and are equipped with information to share with your friends about your 'condition.' Then you become an expert in the disease and associated medication. This is not Father God's solution for your life.

I was a pre-med student when I was young and I dropped out to be a radio DJ. If I

Chapter 2

had gone into medicine I could not help anyone to the degree I have with God. I was a dropout. I was a prodigal son. I was 38 when I was saved. When I came back into the kingdom, I began to understand principles beyond science. Today, I find myself an expert worldwide in my field. I am on the cutting edge of psychiatry and science. How did I get here? I got there because of the Word of God. If you want to defeat depression, begin to read Psalms. Take a chapter a day, and by the end of that book depression will not stand a chance in your life. Do not use the Psalms as a placebo. Do not mechanically read the Psalms with the belief that completing the book as a task will change your life. Use it as life. Use it as truth. Take a lesson from David, who was a man after God's own heart.

> **And when he had removed him, he raised up unto them David to be their king; to whom also he gave testimony, and said, I have found David the *son* of Jesse, a man after mine own heart, which shall fulfil all my will.** Acts 13:22

Yes, he did struggle with his enemies, depression, disease and yet, he was more than a conqueror. Take a lesson from King David. I want to be a man after God's own heart. Do you want to be a man and woman after God's own heart? I do. Why not? I certainly do not want to be a man after the devil's own heart. Yuck.

2 Corinthians 10:5 says, "Holding every thought captive…"

> **Casting down imaginations, and every high thing that exalteth itself against the knowledge of God, and bringing into captivity every thought to the obedience of Christ;**
> 2 Corinthians 10:5

What does it mean to holding every thought captive? It is taking ownership which includes every thought you have, every feeling, every emotion, every picture, everything that surges through your consciousness. Those feelings, apprehensions, and thoughts can cause biological' manifestation to prove you have a problem. You are so easily trapped by the enemy who manipulates your biology. You are a great disciple of error. But you are not called by God to be a disciple of error, you are supposed to be disciples of truth. How do you defeat error? How does error defeat

Depression Impacts Your Spirit, Soul and Body

truth? It is simple. People choose to listen to error. Many of you know the Word of God, and you may make sure everyone else around you knows you do. However, that may not mean you live by the Word as you ought. You can use the Word of God to show the spots and blemishes and the little specs in other people, but what about the beam in your own eye?

> **And why beholdest thou the mote that is in thy brother's eye, but considerest not the beam that is in thine own eye?** Matthew 7:3

God does not want you to become so educated that you do not embrace truth for yourself. First, you need to embrace truth for you and you alone. I have seen so many people trying to help other people in ministry while they themselves were castaways and derelict in truth. Paul said, "What purpose is there if I bring the revelation that God has given me and deep knowledge for mankind and I myself am a castaway?"

> **But I keep under my body, and bring *it* into subjection: lest that by any means, when I have preached to others, I myself should be a castaway.** 1 Corinthians 9:27

What benefit is that? Be selfish. Eat the good manna first. Come on now. I am reasoning with you to reconsider ways of thinking and operating that are not working in your life. I am a life coach.

I am not preaching you a sermon. I am not a preacher. I am an irritator and an agitator. God uses me to compel people to deal with issues and matters in their life they wish I would avoid. To a certain extent, we are happy in our spiritual prison houses. We are like prisoners. It is said that if you take a longtime prisoner, release him to probation and put him back in society, he will commit a crime to return to where it is safe. He cannot stand being free. I see many people, Christians included, that cannot stand being free. They just cannot stand it. They have nothing to talk about and think about, because they have become 'one' with sin. For instance, a person may not just have a spirit of fear, but they have been trained by fear as to what to think and how to behave. While they may hate the consequences of feeling stressed

Chapter 2

and scattered, it is all they know. There is a measure of peace in the predictable patterns of life even though living in fear is tormenting.

Section 2
Spirit-Soul-Body Connection

I want you to understand true freedom. 2 Corinthians 10:5 says, "Casting down imaginations and every high thing that exalts itself against the knowledge of God and bringing into captivity every thought to the obedience of Christ."

Casting down imaginations, and every high thing that exalteth itself against the knowledge of God, and bringing into captivity every thought to the obedience of Christ;

2 Corinthians 10:5

So when thoughts come to you that you are not loved, take hold of those thoughts and ask, "Where did those thoughts come from?"

Spiritual discernment requires examining the origin of thought. Thoughts can originate in your own mind. You can decide to believe a lie that comes to your mind all by yourself. You have an active brain with thoughts popping up all over the place along with feelings and emotions. Your brain is a depository. Everything that you are is recorded in deductive reasoning because of alpha brainwave activity at the cerebral cortex level. Alpha waves allow you to assimilate, tabulate, and condense information to bring into deductive reasoning. This includes the things that you perceive externally through beta, and the things you perceive internally through theta brainwave activity. This is an exact science, folks.

You only have three brainwaves that keep you 'ticking upstairs.' Theta brainwaves are activated audibly at 4 1/2 to 7 drum beats per second. A shaman's drum beat puts a person in a sort of trance making them susceptible to ideas, impressions, and feelings from the enemy. A lack of beta brainwaves would make you a vegetable. On the other hand, if you did not have theta brainwaves you could not hear God. You could not hear the Holy Spirit. He communicates through theta brainwave activity. Without theta, the only way you could experience a witness of truth would require God to physically materialize in this dimension. He would need to communicate with

Depression Impacts Your Spirit, Soul and Body

you through your five physical senses for you to comprehend anything. But God is not going to appear in the physical dimension because He is a spirit.

God *is* a Spirit: and they that worship him must worship *him* in spirit and in truth. John 4:24

He will communicate with you spirit to spirit. For emphasis, I repeat, "God communicates with you spirit to spirit." What you take in through the Word of God by reading it and processing it at the soul level, the Holy Spirit bears witness of the truth at the spirit level. Once you embrace truth spiritually and psychologically, you become one with it. You are no longer double-minded. You understand forgiveness both as a spirit being and also as a psychological human being. You are single minded in conclusion and application. That is what God wants for you. He desires for you to think the same at the spirit man level and the soul level. If you are 'one' in these two dimensions, any spirit that speaks contrary to the Word will be shut down. Your knowledge of God's Word, of which the Holy Spirit has born witness, has formed the basis of your thinking and you will cast down anything opposing it.

Because you are spiritually awake, you will cast down anything that would try to influence you from the spirit world. Your spirit and soul are 'door-points' or gates to the disruption or reclamation of your sanity and spirituality. Regardless of whether beings speak to you externally or internally, you are on duty and awake. You have taken ownership of your life, and you are studying every thought and emotion. To every thought, you will consider: "Where'd that come from? That's not my heart, that's not who I am." But the church has not been taught how to take ownership of their lives. They use Jesus as a placebo. "Well, if Jesus wants me to change he'll just have to do it against my will."

The Word says, "Choose this day what you shall have." You choose this day what you shall have: life or death, blessings or 'blanks'(curses).

I call heaven and earth to record this day against you, *that* I have set before you life and death, blessing and cursing: therefore choose life, that both thou and thy seed may live:

Deuteronomy 30:19

Chapter 2

Who is going to choose? Will Jesus choose for you? In 2 Corinthians 10:6, it indicates it is your choice to obey. It says, "…and having in a readiness to revenge all disobedience when your obedience is fulfilled." That is taking ownership of your life. I am going to defeat thoughts, feelings, and beings that represent disobedience. However, as a prerequisite, we can only defeat disobedience if we make a choice not to practice disobedience. I can only defeat things that are not of God if I obey things that are of God. Are you tracking with me?

And having in a readiness to revenge all disobedience, when your obedience is fulfilled.
2 Corinthians 10:6

I am awake. I am awake every day. The thoughts that come to me are not always good. So what? You might be thinking, "Well, I just wish I wouldn't have these negative, bad thoughts." Flush it. You are not immune to temptation. You are not immune to the influence of a spirit world that wants to get you to listen. So, wake up! You have been listening. You decide what you will embrace as truth. I decide what is not truth. I decide. Even if I have a feeling of rejection, I choose to believe I am not rejected.

If I choose to separate myself from feelings of rejection, I can enjoy my life without the feelings and consequences of following rejection. In this context, 'separation' refers to the concept that I do not have to embrace and accept evil thoughts as my own. Another kingdom is trying to convince me that their thoughts are mine. They are not mine; that is separation. That is your birthright. Because you have a feeling means nothing.

It is good to have good feelings. I do not want you to be a cold, callous robot. It is wonderful to have deep emotions and deep feelings. It is good to have the positive kind and to have empathy, to have love and forgiveness, and patience, and long-suffering. It is good, and God wants you to be the spiritually correct human that He saw from the foundation of the world. His plan for creation did not include sin. There is a kingdom that does not want you to be what God planned.

DEPRESSION IMPACTS YOUR SPIRIT, SOUL AND BODY

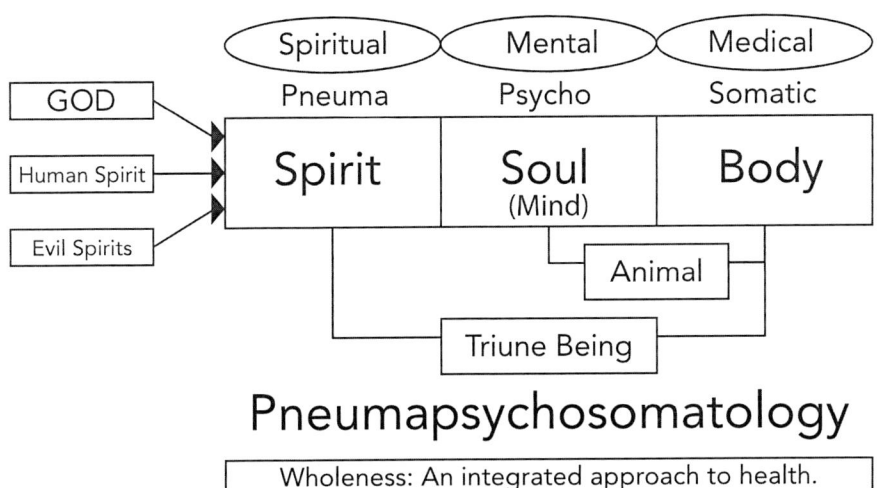

Diagram 2: Pneumapsychosomatology is a term we use to describe the connection between our spirit, soul and body. Humans are triune and our spirit allows us to communicate with God and evil spirits along with our own spirit unlike animals.

To summarize, we are a spirit. we have a soul (our mind), and we have a physical body. The way God, our spirit, and evil spirits speak to us is through theta brainwaves. The way we consider and process thoughts, including our own, occurs through alpha brainwaves. The way we process and receive external stimuli occurs through beta. What if you were not a spirit being? What would you be? Just an animal. That is really how the medical community is treating you–as a biological specimen. Your spirit is inside you, and that is the real you. You are a spirit being. God is a spirit, and He is the Father of what? All spirits.

Furthermore we have had fathers of our flesh which corrected *us*, and we gave *them* reverence: shall we not much rather be in subjection unto the Father of spirits, and live?

Hebrews 12:9

Those that worship Him must worship Him in spirit and what? Lies? No, truth. You need to accept the Word of God as truth for your life and discard everything that contradicts what God has said. The Word says, "Let God be true and every man a liar."

God *is* a Spirit: and they that worship him must worship *him* in spirit and in truth. John 4:24

Chapter 2

That statement is found in the ancient writings, otherwise known as your Bible. I have been using the term 'ancient writings' in conferences lately, because when I use the word 'Bible', people say, "Eh, yeah, okay. I don't care about the Bible." However, when I say ancient writings, they perk up and respond, "Woah, this is good. It is so profound." I am serious; that is how I entice them to reconsider the Word. So lately, I do not use the word Bible. The reason people are intrigued by the term, ancient writings, is that they are more than happy to hear esoteric truth. They want something mysterious and secret.

Many of us have become glazed over to the truth found in something known as the Bible. It is a dust collector on the shelf or a roach haven in the glue of the pages. I want you to defeat the thoughts that are causing a biochemical imbalance, but it requires you to open your Bible and begin to read. I want you to begin the journey of defeating the enemy causing a biochemical imbalance. For the most part at a physical level, all that depression is is the result of biochemical imbalance. Every drug prescribed by psychiatrists deal with either over-secretion or under-secretion of neurotransmitters. That is the pharmacology of all psychiatric medicine. They say there is an imbalance. We have a drug that is inducing a type of biological balance. The Greek term for witchcraft found in Galatians 5 is pharmakeia. Pharmakeia is called a work of the flesh. This is the root word for our modern term pharmaceutical.

> [19] **Now the works of the flesh are manifest, which are** *these*; **Adultery, fornication, uncleanness, lasciviousness,** [20] **Idolatry, witchcraft, hatred, variance, emulations, wrath, strife, seditions, heresies,** [21] **Envyings, murders, drunkenness, revellings, and such like: of the which I tell you before, as I have also told** *you* **in time past, that they which do such things shall not inherit the kingdom of God.**   Galatians 5:19-21

Why are pharmaceutical drugs called a work of the flesh? Because they do not allow you to address the reason your body and mind are malfunctioning. They help you to feel somewhat better rather than removing the core issue preventing you from being normal. I am not against bridging you to freedom. If you temporarily need to take an antidepressant as you learn to apply your heart to the Word until you are no longer dependent on it that is not my concern. I am not against people taking

Depression Impacts Your Spirit, Soul and Body

medication to help bridge them until they can become sanctified. I have this saying, "Keep the sinners alive long enough that I can get them sanctified."

The ultimate goal is for you to no longer need medication. Now God is full of grace and mercy. So I want to make sure that you do not think I am telling you to get off your medication or feel condemned for being on medication. Not at all. But I will tell you that if the need for medication is rooted in not 'holding every thought captive' and embracing anti-Christ and anti-God thoughts they will cause a biochemical imbalance. The medication will manage you with some relief, and that is only a 'half-way house' on the road to freedom. Medications do not produce a cure. I repeat, "Medications do not produce a cure." They are part of the learning curve of application of biblical truth—a 'half-way house.'

Most of the medical profession is running a half-way house between life and death. Trying to 'keep people going' and they consider that God's perfect will. God's perfect will is not to 'keep you going' by managing your health and sanity with a drug. God's perfect will is that you do not have a problem at all. In fact, it is not God's perfect will to heal you. Biblically and theologically, God's perfect will is that you do not get sick at all. If you are sick, you need to know why. Diagnosis is important to me because I cannot see inside your body otherwise. When I am presented with the diagnosis of a physiological problem, I know the beliefs, thoughts, and behaviors causing it. I am very knowledgeable of over a thousand different diseases and disorders. When somebody gives me the name of a syndrome or disease, I know why they have it. I know the etiology. I know the thoughts, and the spirituality and the personality that have caused the body to conform to the image of death instead of life and 'dis-ease' rather than ease. The origin of the problem begins with 'dis-ease' or an underlying lack of ease and peace. Long term, if left undealt with, this will become a diagnosed disease or syndrome. So can we deal with 'dis-ease' before we need to deal with a biological or psychological disease?

Science and the Church have no idea what I am talking about. I am not being critical to destroy or demean them. This is my field. I have been an elder in the Christian church for 30 years, and I have a right to speak into my industry any time I feel like it. I will speak out because God loves you. He does not want to share you with the villain. The gospel offers you more than cohabitation and a half-way house with

Chapter 2

the villain as freedom. Yes, medication and other forms of therapy give a measure of relief, but they are a 'half-way house.' True freedom comes from accepting, believing, and applying the Word to our lives. 'He who the Son makes free is free indeed.'

> **If the Son therefore shall make you free, ye shall be free indeed.** John 8:36

Could we hold out for that possibility? In addressing this issue, your thoughts can come from your own head. Your thoughts can also originate with others who influence you. Fear can be contagious. Gossip can be contagious, but it is 'murder.' Accusation can be contagious. It is 'murder.' Speaking evil of your brother is murder according to Scripture. In the spiritual dimension, accusing and defaming others will result in separation between you and another person including turning people against each other. You are assassinating someone's character when you 'murder them with your words.' It is an attempt to assassinate their character.

> **But I say unto you, That whosoever is angry with his brother without a cause shall be in danger of the judgment: and whosoever shall say to his brother, Raca, shall be in danger of the council: but whosoever shall say, Thou fool, shall be in danger of hell fire.**
> Matthew 5:22

Do we read the Word for our sanity and our safety? You can be influenced by people around you. If you are influenced by what others have convinced you to think, speak, and act, it is transferred into your soul (mind) and you now have a fixation of persona or personality. On the other hand, the Holy Spirit wants to influence you. The Holy Spirit influences you by undergirding the Word of God. You have two paths to choose. Either you will choose to read and believe the Word of God or choose to make other people, with their correct or incorrect opinions, the source of your decisions.

> **Howbeit when he, the Spirit of truth, is come, he will guide you into all truth: for he shall not speak of himself; but whatsoever he shall hear, *that* shall he speak: and he will shew you things to come.** John 16:13

Depression Impacts Your Spirit, Soul and Body

'God watches over His Word to perform it' implementing truth is the work of the Holy Spirit. But Satan and his kingdom, the bureaucracy he oversees in Ephesians chapter 6, want to influence you, too.

For we wrestle not against flesh and blood, but against principalities, against powers, against the rulers of the darkness of this world, against spiritual wickedness in high places. Ephesians 6:12

Paul said this in Romans 7, "I want to do good, but I don't do it and the good that I wish I would do, I don't do it. The evil that I wish I would not do, that's what I do." Then Paul said, "In the day that I do this evil that I wish I would not do, it is no longer I that do it, but sin that dwells in me."

[15] For that which I do I allow not: for what I would, that do I not; but what I hate, that do I. [16] If then I do that which I would not, I consent unto the law that *it is* good. [17] Now then it is no more I that do it, but sin that dwelleth in me. [18] For I know that in me (that is, in my flesh,) dwelleth no good thing: for to will is present with me; but *how* to perform that which is good I find not. Romans 7:15-18

What he is saying is that he has been influenced by sin that lives within to get him to think, speak, and act differently than what God intended. Even though he knows God's Word and he says amen to it, there is another war in his members that is warring against the law of his mind bringing him into captivity to the law of sin. Thankfully, there is a solution and Paul does not leave us with a fatalistic conclusion. 'O Retched man that I am. Who shall deliver me from this body of death? Well, I thank God through Jesus Christ our Lord. There are possibilities for freedom. So then with the mind I myself serve the law of God; but with the flesh the law of sin.'

[19] For the good that I would I do not: but the evil which I would not, that I do. [20] Now if I do that I would not, it is no more I that do it, but sin that dwelleth in me. [21] I find then a law, that, when I would do good, evil is present with me. [22] For I delight in the law of God after the inward man: [23] But I see another law in my members, warring against the law of my mind, and bringing me into captivity to the law of sin which is in my members. [24] O

Chapter 2

wretched man that I am! who shall deliver me from the body of this death? [25] I thank God through Jesus Christ our Lord. So then with the mind I myself serve the law of God; but with the flesh the law of sin. Romans 7:19-25

CHAPTER 3:
THE CONNECTION BETWEEN RELATIONSHIPS AND DEPRESSION

Following wrong thoughts can disrupt your peace. God has made you to live in peace. It is necessary to calm down. You need to lower dopamine, bring the serotonin up, come out of fight or flight and get the norepinephrine back to normal. We might produce a chemistry balance today and enjoy the peace of God in our hearts. What do you think? Did you know you could control your biochemistry? Absolutely. In 2 Corinthians 10:5, it says you are to hold every thought captive.

Casting down imaginations, and every high thing that exalteth itself against the knowledge of God, and bringing into captivity every thought to the obedience of Christ;

2 Corinthians 10:5

By 'casting down every imagination' that cause your serotonin levels to dip, your serotonin levels will soar. In turn, that would cause your dopamine levels to dip, because 'vain imaginations' cause your dopamine levels to soar. You may be thinking, "Is it that simple?" In about 80% of all depression cases, yes it is. Now we can address every individual, isolated syndrome and phobia, but we would lose the point of this teaching in the midst of a separate dialogue. We need to keep focused because I intend to leave you with an impression that you will never forget. You do not have to have depression!

However, if you do not play by the principles of the kingdom of God and His Word, and what He says about you, then you are going to listen to another kingdom who will reform you into some other image. I want to discuss manic depression and the larger subject of mood disorders. Manic depression is also known as bipolar

Chapter 3

disorder. Let me insert a word in your thinking; it is the term 'psychopathological'. Pathology is the study of disease. That is what a pathologist does.

When I was a pre-med student, I was a guest of a doctor in Louisville, Kentucky every weekend. I was handpicked to be a doctor in American. I had the aptitude and everything going for me. Two of the doctors on the board of directors of the University of Louisville Medical School were my mentors. One was a surgeon, and the other was the head pathologist for the city of Louisville. I will never forget the times I spent with the pathologist every other weekend going into the catacombs of the hospital in the pathology department and looking at all of the organs in jars of formaldehyde. When they did an autopsy, they would remove the organ that was the reason for death. I will never forget looking at cancer of the liver. It was a beautiful thing. Now, do not take my statement the wrong way. It is not a beautiful thing to have cancer of the liver. However, where the cancer was, there were bright circles of blues and pinks and yellows. It looked as if an artist went in there and put blobs of paint. It was startling to say the least. These experiences helped to form my understanding and thought process around the topic of pathology.

So I would like to insert the word pathology and also include the words 'somatic expression'. What is a somatic expression? The term 'soma' refers to our body. Therefore, it is an expression at the physical level of our existence. Now, I am not trying to be overly technical. I simply want to define certain terms to establish a foundation for your understanding. The next word I want to insert into this conversation is 'psychogenic'. The word psychogenic means to have its origin in thought. It is the foundation of the mind-body connection. Science has known for a long time that thought can produce syndromes and diseases. The church does not understand nor has it been taught that. So we are still in the dark ages theologically and scientifically. We ask God to help us in our ignorance and lack of knowledge. It is sad, because these principles are simple. What I am teaching you is very basic and very simple, not complicated. It is down to earth which is where we should land and be of some earthly good rather than tormented and distracted by sin.

So psychopathology refers to thoughts that create a biological manifestation. What are moods? Moods are sustained emotions. Now they can be short term, or, if you focus on them, they can be longer and longer and longer. The more that you

The Connection Between Relationships & Depression

stay in that mood or the thoughts that produce that mood, the greater the chance of that thought, mood, or emotion becoming part of your long term memory. It is very possible, because you are being trained, to be moody. You are being trained in thought so that your body will constantly respond to your mind. Your bodies are responders. Your body does not think. All of your God-given body systems from your gastrointestinal to neurological to your central nervous system function to keep you moving; every single one is susceptible to thought.

An important example of how thoughts affect our bodies can be found in the general adaptation syndrome of fear, anxiety, and stress. It explains how just one stressor can control your body and produce various issues. I did not make up what I am sharing. This is coming right out of general medicine. It is taught in medical schools, but when you visit your doctor he has forgotten what he learned. Why? Because pharmaceutical companies do not want you to know what your doctor learned. You might get well and not need their product. I do not know if you are aware of this, but pharmaceutical companies have influence within medical schools because they have the money for research. [14, 15] Without the truth you are being taught, there are no real solutions. Instead, pharmaceutical companies offer alternative forms of peace and disease management by manipulating your biochemistry.

Do you know that pharmaceutical companies are now making drugs for well people? The drug industry for our youth, ages three years old and up, is a rapidly growing market for drug companies because they have not experienced acceptance and love. They have performance and drivenness. The educational demand for our youth is 'straight A's' and anything less means you are defective. Then we put pressure on all our kids to be 'straight A' students. God never intended that all of mankind be white collar. There is no stigma to blue collar work. So get out of your cast system. Get out of the programming of elitism. Education and intelligence do not make anyone superior to anyone else. Every body part in the body of Christ is important even the ones you cannot see. In fact, the Bible states that the uncomely parts have more value than the comely.

---

14. Kluger, Jeffrey. "Is Drug-Company Money Tainting Medical Education?" Time. Time Inc., 06 Mar. 2009. Web. 24 Apr. 2017

15. Wilson, Duff. "Harvard Medical School in Ethics Quandary." The New York Times. The New York Times, 02 Mar. 2009. Web. 24 Apr. 2017

Chapter 3

> **And those *members* of the body, which we think to be less honourable, upon these we bestow more abundant honour; and our uncomely *parts* have more abundant comeliness.**
>
> 1 Corinthians 12:23

Did you not read that in your Bible? Quit looking at yourself like you are a vestigial appendage or a dangling participle of no use to the body.

I am the intestine in the body of Christ. I just love being the intestine. In the body of Christ, I am the intestine because I help you process spiritual nutrients and waste to discern what thoughts and ideas are nourishing and what needs to be removed. Besides my functions as an elder of the church, anyone that has known me over the years knows that all that I do as a body part, and have done since I was born again, is help people process 'spiritual' food and get rid of waste. You need a guy like me. I like being the intestine; I get to eat first and get relieved first. If you did not have an intestine that properly functioned, you would be goofy. Thank God for a functioning gastrointestinal system—even of the spiritual variety.

Now, I know perhaps it would not thrill you to talk about your intestine on the front page, but it is an essential part of you. Regardless of what you are called to do in the body of Christ, you must remember that 'God has placed those in the church as it has pleased Him.'

> **But now hath God set the members every one of them in the body, as it hath pleased him.**
>
> 1 Corinthians 12:18

Why not just accept it? Quit comparing yourself to others. That is enough to cause you to have depression. Besides, when you start to pattern yourself after somebody else, you are about to emulate their incompetence. They may have strengths, but they also have weaknesses you may copy. There has to be something better for you than somebody else's level of competence or incompetence. When you look at others and compare yourself to them, you disregard that God is the one that created you and He is the one that saved you. Relax in it–just relax.

Moods are sustained emotions. If we learn to look to God the effects of emotions are more short-lived expressions rather than long-term moods. In our process of learning to look to God, we dip in and out of temptation. We dip in and out of feelings. When we dip in and out of moods and feelings, they may have some latent ability to create temporary biological responses, but they are not as dangerous as long term fixation. If you enter into long-term fixation, you enter into fear based, phobic fixation. All phobias are learned behaviors. We did a one day conference on a phobic fixation called Post-traumatic stress disorder or PTSD. All phobias are learned behaviors. Long term mood profiles are also learned behaviors. So if the things that make you phobic and depressed are the result of long-term learned behaviors, should it not also be possible to unlearn these behaviors? That is why you embrace the law of God to combat the law of sin.

For the law of the Spirit of life in Christ Jesus hath made me free from the law of sin and death. Romans 8:2

The apostle Paul, born-again, filled with the Holy Ghost, an apostle of the church, bluntly states that in his members he has two laws.

[22] For I delight in the law of God after the inward man: [23] But I see another law in my members, warring against the law of my mind, and bringing me into captivity to the law of sin which is in my members. Romans 7:22-23

We pretend we do not because if we admit there are 'bats in our belfry tower' ,we are afraid others will not like us. But these spiritual problems are already manifesting. Everything that is not of God, in a human will manifest sometime in their lifetime–usually at the worst time to do the most damage. So if that is the case then everything that is of God, should also manifest at some point in our lifetime. So what is manifesting in us? What is manifesting out of us? Out of our thoughts, out of our speech, out of our actions? Which kingdom is manifesting? For some, they swing from depression to elation; that is an emotional roller coaster. Depression to elation is what manifests in manic depression. That would be the peaks and valleys of mood changes. So, you go from the pit of despair to grandiose highs.

Now, sadness and joy can be part of the fabric of everyday life, but when

Chapter 3

maintained in extremes they are problematic. If you stayed effusive and overly happy all the time, I do not know if I could stand you. Please, calm down. Now I know it is okay to be happy, but not chandelier swinging, intense jubilation. You will make me nervous because that would be extreme, would it not? Most people that act happy all the time to the extreme, usually have an anxiety disorder. People that talk a lot are usually afraid of people. So you have the extremes and their consequences. Can we find a midrange where you do not have to fall into the gully of despair or hang out on the clouds every day? Can we just find a place of peace? The Word is very clear that 'perfect peace belongs to those whose minds are fixed or stayed on the Lord.'

> **Thou wilt keep *him* in perfect peace, *whose* mind is stayed on *thee*: because he trusteth in thee.**   Isaiah 26:3

Who is the Lord in this scripture? God the Word. If you do not know the Word of God, also known as the Bible, you are going to have no peace. You do not have any resources to maintain it. If you do not know what God says in the Bible you have nothing to apply to your life situations. Instead, it will be human and humanistic. It will be psychic, the result of Satan's kingdom giving you thoughts. It will be an emulation of others. It will be a fabricated, presumptuous solution. We have enough fabricated personalities already, please 'flush it.' Just be you.

Maybe you do not know who you are. That is a sad reality. Do you know how many people I talk to that do not know who they are? They are in a vacant world. I know they have a driver's license and they have a name, but that is about all they know about themselves. I am sure you run across people with fabricated personalities. It is yucky. Yuck! Who needs it? That is why we need to know God's Word and believe what Father God says about us and our value.

Section 1
Insights into Specific Conditions
Bipolar/Manic Depression

Bipolar disorder is alternating episodes of depression and elation. This differs from unipolar. You do not hear the word unipolar very often, but it only involves an ongoing state of depression, including perhaps melancholy. It is a straight line of constancy. Returning to the subject of bipolar, it usually begins before the age of 25.[16] 18 to 25 is the average age range that people start developing bipolar personalities.[17] Interestingly enough, it is also the same age range as those who develop paranoid schizophrenia.[18] Now, although they do see evidence of genetic markers on the X chromosome possibly linked to manic depression/bipolar,[19] they have not isolated a genetic marker inherited in paranoid schizophrenia. On a practical level, what normally occurs in a person's life between the ages of 18 and 25? Normally a person is emerging from puberty into young adulthood and independence. However, from what I have observed, in the cases of bipolar and paranoid schizophrenia this dynamic is askew. These individuals are living in an upside down world rather than transitioning from dependence to independence.

Dependency can also be found in abusive families. It is a dependency on abuse. There are people that, in adulthood, try to find someone that will abuse them even though they would deny it. Inside they love it and they are drawn to it because they have inherited the desire to be abused. This is a classic, typical situation. It explains how many females go back to an abusive husband, because they are co-dependent with him. Time and time again they are beaten.

For those attempting to treat these issues medically, hypomania, which is an elevated mood of elation, may be triggered by administration of antidepressants.[20]

---

14. Kluger, Jeffrey. "Is Drug-Company Money Tainting Medical Education?" Time. Time Inc., 06 Mar. 2009. Web. 24 Apr. 2017

16. Anderson IM, Haddad PM, Scott J (Dec 27, 2012). "Bipolar disorder". BMJ (Clinical research ed.). 345: e8508. doi:10.1136/bmj.e8508. PMID 23271744

17. Christie KA, Burke JD Jr, Regier DA, Rae DS, Boyd JH, Locke BZ: Epidemiologic evidence for early onset of mental disorders and higher risk of drug abuse in young adults. Am J Psychiatry 1988; 145:971–975

18. Sham, P. C., C. J. MacLean, and K. S. Kendler. "A Typological Model of Schizophrenia Based on Age at Onset, Sex and Familial Morbidity." Acta Psychiatrica Scandinavica. U.S. National Library of Medicine, Feb. 1994. Web. 24 Apr. 2017

19. Kendler KS, Karkowski LM, Walsh D (1998) The structure of psychosis. Arch Gen Psychiatry 55:492–499

20. Terao, Takeshi, and Teruaki Tanaka. "Antidepressant-induced Mania or Hypomania in DSM-5." SpringerLink. Springer Berlin Heidelberg, 19 Nov. 2013. Web. 24 Apr. 2017

Chapter 3

So what are you going to do with that one? You did not have this new condition until you took a drug.

Manic depression can also run in your families. There can be a bipolar family history. Additionally, there may be a three generation active pedigree, where every person for three straight generations has bipolar disorder in their family tree. Again, it can be an inherited genetic issue. The hypomania, as part of the profile, shows up in a person being driven, ambitious, and achievement oriented but to excess. It is a fixation on achievement. Instead of growing into success gradually, they are driven and pushed for success. God is not going to drive you to success. It may take years to grow up into it, but the devil will try to drive you into success and that is ungodly. Be careful of your motivation.

Many diseases have a psychosomatic origin. We do not like that fact, because we want to believe there is no problem in our heads. No, we may have a problem in our spirit, and our head just got in the way. We do not like the word psychosomatic, because it bothers us. You can say we have a horrible physical disease, but do not suggest we have a problem in our heads. There is a stigma attached to it. From over twenty years of experience, I have found specific patterns and ways of dealing with depression are common to certain cultures and races of people. I have found listening to guilty rumination and stewing on guilt and self-reproach are more characteristic of depression in the Anglo-Saxon cultures. I have perceived that people of Anglo-Saxon extractions and backgrounds, who struggle with depression are prone to guilt and self-accusation and self-reproach.

On the other hand, I have found different patterns of depression among those people originating from some Mediterranean and African countries. This group includes those whose generations are historically from those regions and Africa in particular. More often, I have observed a greater tendency toward mania than classic depression amongst these people groups. Mania is a form of depression because it involves a drivenness that is never satisfied. A black hole that is never filled. This need can drive a man to look for love in all of the wrong places including problems like adultery. He can have a perfectly fine, beautiful wife and yet he is never satisfied. He is looking for other women anywhere he can find them. That is a form of depression. It is a drivenness to get a dopamine rush, a feel good experience. He is looking for

THE CONNECTION BETWEEN RELATIONSHIPS & DEPRESSION

the excitement that comes with being noticed by a female because he is down and feels depressed. He needs to feel a rush to compensate for this deficiency. 'She noticed me; I'm special.' He goes to Walmart, and his eyes are seeking out any female that may notice him. That is a depressed state. There is a void that needs to be filled. I hope you are tracking with me. When one of these guys looks at a lady, she may feel yucky because of this ungodly need. People in these situations are at higher risk for psychiatric conditions such as depression and anxiety disorders, schizophrenic disorders, an early phase of cortical dementia, antisocial personality, alcoholism, and other substance abuse disorders.

Heredity is the most important predisposing factor. These family trees are comprised of generations of those that have not felt loved. The number one door point for all depression is the inability of a male to be a proper covering as a father and a husband. A poor relationship between a father and child keeps you from accepting God the Father because He has the name 'father.' In many parts of Christianity, they center around Jesus, and it is all about Jesus to the exclusion of the Father. Jesus came to show us the Father—Father God. You need to accept that Father God loves you. Instead, the church is Jesus-centric. They do not realize Jesus himself said, "I came to show you the Father."

> **8 Philip saith unto him, Lord, shew us the Father, and it sufficeth us. 9 Jesus saith unto him, Have I been so long time with you, and yet hast thou not known me, Philip? he that hath seen me hath seen the Father; and how sayest thou *then*, Shew us the Father?** John 14:8-9

I do not mean to be disrespectful to the Lord Jesus. However, we need to set in order the Godhead. The Godhead is comprised of Father God, God the Word, who is Jesus, and the Holy Spirit. Father God is the head of the Godhead, not Jesus. Jesus did not instruct us to ask him for what we need. 'All good things come down from the Father of Lights above, with whom is no variableness of turning.'

> **Every good gift and every perfect gift is from above, and cometh down from the Father of lights, with whom is no variableness, neither shadow of turning.** James 1:17

Chapter 3

Jesus taught them as well as us to pray saying, "Our Father who art in heaven."

After this manner therefore pray ye: Our Father which art in heaven, Hallowed be thy name. Matthew 6:9

In John 16, Jesus said, "In that day you should ask me nothing but you shall ask the Father in my name, and He shall give to you whatsoever you ask."

And in that day ye shall ask me nothing. Verily, verily, I say unto you, Whatsoever ye shall ask the Father in my name, he will give *it* you. John 16:23

What prevents us from going to God the Father is our belief that He never smiles. Religion has made Him unkind, unfeeling, and unsmiling. Jesus said, "If you have seen me, you have seen the Father. I only think and speak like my Father."

[10] Believest thou not that I am in the Father, and the Father in me? the words that I speak unto you I speak not of myself: but the Father that dwelleth in me, he doeth the works. [11] Believe me that I *am* in the Father, and the Father in me: or else believe me for the very works' sake. John 14:10-11

What happened to the rest of us sons and daughters? I am asking a very direct question, because we need to reconsider our position. So what happened to the rest of us sons and daughters? Why do we act differently than Jesus? He was a Son of God, was he not? Was Jesus the Son of God? Son of man? Was he acquainted with sorrow and grief? Did he die for our sins as a human? Did he have feelings? Yes. However, did he blame it on his Father in heaven? Did he blame it on himself? No, he knew who to blame—the devil. And he knew who to glorify—the Father!

There are several forms of depression. Unipolar is a straight line form of depression without the highs of mania. This form of depression is more likely to rise from a background of introversion and an anxious, neurotic tendency. Inversion, self-centeredness, self-introspection, and self-accusation are the enemies of someone struggling with unipolar issues. Additionally, these spirits are coupled with shame and guilt. Self-pity is the glue that holds it all together. If you have self-pity and you

The Connection Between Relationships & Depression

struggle with it, you have no faith whatsoever, because self-pity always reflects the failure of something from the past. Constantly reliving the past binds your present to past failures. Faith requires hope that God can give you a new future irrespective of your past.

There are only about three chemicals that are used to treat bipolar/manic depression. They are HCAs or TCAs. They increase the availability of norepinephrine and serotonin by blocking reuptake. Prozac is similar to these drugs. People that have depression and manic depression/bipolar always have a lowered level of serotonin. Serotonin makes you feel better. Satan's kingdom suppresses your body from producing this chemical that gives you a 'feel good' feeling about yourself. They feed you negative thoughts and then you choose to continue to put yourself down. As you continue listening to accusation about your value through the mind-body connection, you devalue your identity.

Paranoid Schizophrenia

I want to help you understand Paranoid Schizophrenia by explaining the biological mechanisms behind it. To begin with, Paranoid Schizophrenia is not really a disease. There is not one thing wrong with the human brain in Paranoid Schizophrenia. The problem lies in what is causing the over secretion of dopamine and norepinephrine. Norepinephrine is the fight or flight of paranoia in this profile. Biologically Paranoid Schizophrenia is a result of the over secretion of two neurotransmitters. If we could stop these transmitters from over secreting norepinephrine and dopamine guess what would happen? You would no longer have Schizophrenia, and the person's mind would be at peace.

1 John 4:18 establishes an important foundation for overcoming Paranoid Schizophrenia.

> **There is no fear in love; but perfect love casteth out fear: because fear hath torment. He that feareth is not made perfect in love.** 1 John 4:18

I discovered that Paranoid Schizophrenia usually develops between 18 and 25 and follows certain family trees. People who developed it grew up in families

Chapter 3

that did not know how to love each other or worse their value was performance orientated. In other words, the child's value was how well he or she did something. The only time the child was accepted was when they did things perfectly because failure was unacceptable. It was horrible when they failed. So they ended up in fight or flight concerning the parent that put that on them.

God never intended for everybody to get 'straight A's' in school. In my home, I have always had a rule concerning grades. In fact, I helped one of my children years ago, avoid a psychiatric disease when I refused to let him be A+ orientated to compete with his friends. I told him, "You're going to be a great student, but you may not be an A+ student. So what? Here's the deal, A, B, and C's are acceptable. D's and F's are not. Do the best you can."

In releasing my son from that peer pressure and pressure of performance, he not only came out of the psychosis that was forming, he also lost 20 pounds of weight. When he was stuck in the mindset of not liking himself, his rate of metabolism slowed down, caloric burned slowed down, he was chubby, and it made him hate himself even more. So when he had a reality check from proper fatherly instruction, and he began to understand what I was saying and apply it, he lost 20 pounds and got out of that pathway of psychosis.

Today he is a great son living in Seattle, Washington. He is an anesthesiologist. He has a beautiful wife, four gorgeous children, loves God, and is brilliant. When he was younger he was one of three people in all of the United States to be chosen by the government to become an anesthesiologist.

He got his doctorate in Be In Health® principles on the subject of how thoughts effect your body. That was his doctorate. He got an A on that paper. He was saved from a lot of problems because of proper knowledge. All those years back, I had to release him from drivenness and competition. In today's world of business, it is all about competition. In sports, it is a competition. In business, it is a competition. No wonder we have so many diseases, but this is how it comes.

Understanding Paranoid Schizophrenia from a biblical perspective requires an exploration of 1 John 4:18. In 1 John 4:18, there are four very important parts.

> **There is no fear in love; but perfect love casteth out fear: because fear hath torment. He that feareth is not made perfect in love.** 1 John 4:18

THE CONNECTION BETWEEN RELATIONSHIPS & DEPRESSION

First of all, 'there is no fear in love.' If you do not feel loved, guess what is coming to you? Fear. Fear produces isolation and withdraw. You hibernate. You withdraw. You do not want to be around people. They make you afraid. They make you sweat, make you nervous, and make you 'twitchy.' You develop sweats, tremors, and nervous stomach, because you are afraid someone might reject you. So you withdraw because you do not feel loved. You do not feel accepted.

Fear has torment. Fear is the issue behind Paranoid Schizophrenia. 'God has not given you the spirit of fear but power, love, and a sound mind.'

For God hath not given us the spirit of fear; but of power, and of love, and of a sound mind. 2 Timothy 1:7

If you have fear, you are not going to have any power of action to move forward. You are not going to feel loved, and you are not going to have soundness of mind. That is pretty serious, is it not? So it has torment. This torment is a part of the profile of Paranoid Schizophrenia. I consider it not just a phobic disorder, but a depression disorder because it involves withdrawal and isolation.

The next part of 1 John 4:18 is that 'he that fears is not made perfect in love.'

There is no fear in love; but perfect love casteth out fear: because fear hath torment. He that feareth is not made perfect in love. 1 John 4:18

What does that mean? If a person has this kind of fear, they are not able to give and receive love without fear. They cannot care for or be cared for by others, and they are unable to receive love from others. When someone gets close to them, they push that person away. So how do you deal with it? Well, 1 John 4:18 has the antidote. 'Perfect love casts out fear.'

There is no fear in love; but perfect love casteth out fear: because fear hath torment. He that feareth is not made perfect in love. 1 John 4:18

If you want to help people that are struggling with their identity and have depressive episodes, start loving them. I know they are hard to get along with.

Chapter 3

Who asked you to only get along with people that are agreeable and nice? Even the heathen can do that. Even the heathen get along with people that get along with them. That is not proof of your spirituality. '

Well, I only want to hang out with normal people.' The truth is there are no normal people! We all have our stuff and issues, do we not? Some are obvious and the rest we are in denial about, but everybody in our life knows they are there anyway. However, if we remember that 'perfect love casts out fear' we can help those who are struggling in our lives.

I was teaching about Paranoid Schizophrenia in Minnesota years ago when a man came up to me, and he said, "Wow. I have two brothers. One has already committed suicide. The other brother should be in the lockup, and he has one foot in and one foot out right now. He has Paranoid Schizophrenia. Both of my brothers had Paranoid Schizophrenia. Are you suggesting that if I loved my brother that the fear that caused the disorder would be driven out of him?" I said, "I'm not suggesting that at all. It's what the Word says. It says, 'Perfect love casts out fear.'"

There is no fear in love; but perfect love casteth out fear: because fear hath torment. He that feareth is not made perfect in love. 1 John 4:18

Well, I did not hear anything about him after that. A year and a half later I was in Garland, Texas and this guy showed up with an incredible testimony. He drove all the way from Minnesota to Texas just to give me this testimony. This is powerful, folks. He said, "I decided that if the Word of God was true and you were right on, rather than avoiding my brother, I would visit him. I'd been avoiding him because he was difficult and wasn't making any sense. I couldn't hang out with him because he was out there in this weird world. But, I decided that I'd give this a shot because I loved my brother anyway. Every Saturday I would give him two to three hours of my time to find some place of communication with him. Every week I did that for one year."

In one year, he began to interact with his brother without telling him to 'get it together and stop acting out.' When you tell these people to get it together and stop acting out, they will become worse. You are driving them right into isolation, and paranoia, and avoidance. If they could stop doing it, they would. So it is not by

The Connection Between Relationships & Depression

command. It is according to knowledge. He said, "As I began to spend Saturdays with my brother, he became calmer and calmer and calmer. Pastor, I need to tell you what happened in a year. At the end of one year, I have a brother that is in his right mind. He is on no medications. He is engaged to be married, holds a full-time job very successfully, and is healed without medical intervention." He said, "The Word of God is true that perfect love cast out fear."

God's Word did what medical science could not. Let me explain some details of Paranoid Schizophrenia. We are talking about neurotransmitters and how susceptible humans are to thought. Paranoid Schizophrenia is a compound disorder. It involves Paranoia and what is called 'Schizo' or splitting of the human personality. 'Schizo' means splitting. It involves the oversecretion of norepinephrine. When you find norepinephrine being over-secreted, there is fight or flight. The central nervous system is affected. The fight or flight response of the Paranoid Schizophrenia profile begins with a young person that does not feel safe in their family either, because of abuse or drivenness to perform. It is a stressor. Who they are is how well they do something and, in some instances, they could not do anything right at all. Maybe there was physical abuse or verbal abuse. Perhaps it was emotional abuse. There are many profiles and case histories of people that go either way here, but the result is the same—they must escape. That creates a phobia. That is fight or flight. Biologically and chemically to be sustained in that fight of flight, norepinephrine has to be released to put them in that state.

Now let us discuss the role of dopamine. Dopamine is the pleasure neurotransmitter of the body. A person with Paranoid Schizophrenia has to disassociate and check out of situations to create a safe place. This place in their mind is where you cannot harm them. To stay in that elevated, sustained state of existence then dopamine has to be released to give them feelings of pleasure. They think you are nuts and they are sane. There is a lot that this psychosis can come with and it can be very dangerous. Suicide and other problems are a consequence of this condition, and I am not suggesting that initially putting them on a pharmaceutical drug as a form of intervention is a bad thing. It may calm them down. It can serve as a bridge to help them to deal with immediate symptoms. However, it may not be wisdom to keep them on medication long term because psychiatric drugs also carry with them consequences. I have to tell you that psychiatric drugs that are being given long term become a part of their biology and the body now demands it as a normal routine. To come off of these drugs, there is a lot withdrawal, because the body says, "What are you doing? I need this chemical for me to function." So we have this biochemical fixation that forms.

There are certain drugs that become a part of your body, and they are very difficult to detox. Neurontin is one of the worst drugs on the market today. I call it the 'new rotten' drug. It is being used for everything from toothaches to indigestion. It was developed for epilepsy, and it is being used for many reasons far beyond epilepsy.[21] We are in trouble.

If you have someone that has Paranoid Schizophrenia, there is nothing wrong with their brain. But you have to go back and look at what took them down the journey to become phobic and to isolate in a world of delusional thinking. Now, if you help somebody that is 'up' in mania, it is a repressive state, but the mania also involves a phobic element. If someone is engulfed in mania, then they are going to have what we call 'the voices.' These are the hallucinatory voices that they hear. That is a high-level stress disorder driven with auditory manifestations. It is coming out of the escape mechanism of paranoid schizophrenia. All that the world does is incarcerate these people and put them on drugs. Many are in mental institutions never to come out when all they needed was love to begin with. We are in the 'dark ages.' A lot of people deal with it as only a demonic issue. Just cast their devils out, and they will be sane. I wish it were that easy. It is not 'just' a devil. It is a fixation of personality. Even if there was an evil spirit and you cast it out, you still have the retraining of the human mind to trust others. The only way you can defeat paranoid schizophrenia is that the person has to trust somebody again.

In the case of the brothers, the one with the problem had to begin to trust his brother. As he began to trust, then he was no longer in fight or flight. Because he began to trust, he was no longer disassociating to escape. From a clinical standpoint, I have to describe what happened in this case. The oversecretion of norepinephrine

---

21. Eguale, Tewodros, David L. Buckeridge, Aman Verma, Nancy E. Winslade, Andrea Benedetti, James A. Hanley, and Robyn Tamblyn. "Association of Off-label Drug Use and Adverse Drug Events in an Adult Population." JAMA Internal Medicine 176.1 (2016): 55. Web

The Connection Between Relationships & Depression

and the over re-uptake of dopamine began to subside and subside until his biochemistry in those two dimensions were normal, and he no longer wanted to run. He no longer wanted to disassociate. He was happy to be a part of society. That is a miracle! But what I want to emphasize is that there was an application involved. Even the person that was out there with paranoid schizophrenia had to open his heart. That is why 'perfect love casts out fear' that they can open their heart because well past the mental and biological fixation there is a human that lives inside called a 'spirit being.' That is where the Holy Spirit is located. If we take the perspective of psychiatry, we will miss the spiritual component. If we believe that the treatment and healing of psychiatric problems is a clinical exercise of administering drugs, we will not realize that the human spirit has to be retrained. In fact, if we do not address it from 'within,' then we have lost the battle entirely. You have to consider the whole man: spirit, soul, and body.

Besides Prozac, TCAs and monoamine oxidase inhibitors are the main antidepressants. They are not prescribed often because of their conflicting action with other chemicals or foods. Lithium is another antidepressant. Lithium is a metal. It is a naturally occurring alkali metal. Now, and I am just conjecturing, if lithium is alkali is it possible that a person in depression becomes acidic? I have to explain something I know. Anxiety will make a human acidic. A person that has their peace with others, God, and themselves will have a proper alkaline foundation of biochemistry. So if you want to be acidic, then stew on negative thoughts and feelings. Be anxious for everything. Be phobic, and you will find yourself being a possible candidate for this. According to research I found, the reason is unknown as to why lithium works in stabilizing the unpredictable, often explosive, mood swings and behavior of bipolar. They have no idea how it works. Because it works, doctors give it and it seems to calm you down.

I suppose that if we could break the overly acidic part of human biochemistry, you might calm down because you would not be living in fight or flight. That is just something to consider. Lithium has no effect on normal mood. Why? Because in a normal mood you are not acidic. If you have a normal mood and your personality is normal you are going to have a biochemistry balance and your pH value is going to be doing pretty well. You are not going to be too alkaline. You are not going to

Chapter 3

be too acidic. You are going to have a biochemistry balance. Is that not what God intended?

I have studied this subject with some level of interest to understand how this works. It has also been observed that if levels of serotonin are depressed, it can have a consequence on other chemicals. This increases the susceptibility of norepinephrine, serotonin, and dopamine to thoughts, emotions, and feelings causing these neurotransmitters to be suppressed and/or increased in volume. Thus under secretion of these neurotransmitters can produce a wide range of physiological responses. Additionally, the oversecretion of these neurotransmitters can produce another range of responses such as Paranoid Schizophrenia.

Let me explain how simple fear and anxiety can affect your physiology. Fear is not biological. Fear involves thoughts, and feelings, and emotions. Would you agree with that? Fear does not originate in your psychology, either. Fear is a spirit that answers to Satan. We know that from one Scripture: 'God has not given us the spirit of fear but power, love, and a sound mind.'

> **For God hath not given us the spirit of fear; but of power, and of love, and of a sound mind.** 2 Timothy 1:7

You can also find fear in the book of Job. A spirit of fear manifested and the hair on a man's arm went straight up in the air.

> **[14] Fear came upon me, and trembling, which made all my bones to shake. [15] Then a spirit passed before my face; the hair of my flesh stood up:** Job 4:14-15

We can get into all kinds of stories and various types of manifestations. However, more importantly, fear can impact us in a variety of ways. Fear affects the cardiovascular system, the muscles, the connective tissue, pulmonary system, immune system, gastrointestinal, all the way down to central nervous system, and depression may also be a byproduct of unresolved fear. If you do not feel people love you and you have a phobia that others will not love you, these are the ingredients for depression. It is rooted in perceived or real rejection and isolation and withdrawal, which requires fear to fueling these thoughts and feelings. In many instances, people

The Connection Between Relationships & Depression

have been rejected by those who were supposed to love them. They not only feel rejected, but take in a spirit of rejection and a spirit of fear, because they feel afraid and isolated. Once a person is trained to believe this pattern of life will continue, they are stuck in a vicious cycle. So there you have depression.

Section 2
True Diseases Versus 'Sin-Dromes'

Now, disease is broken down in two ways. A true biological disease involves organic damage of body systems and the resulting symptoms and issues. Syndromes differ in that symptoms and issues manifest because something is disrupting the proper function of body systems, but there is no evidence of organic damage. For example, Hyperthyroidism is a true disease in which the immune attacks your thyroid destroying the tissue. On the other hand, Hypothyroidism is a syndrome because nothing is wrong with your thyroid, but something spiritual is interfering with its proper function. Diabetes type I is a true disease in which the immune system begins to attack the body. Diabetes II is an anxiety disorder; there is nothing wrong with the body at all.

A true disease is defined as a condition impacting bodily functions as a result of damage. But when the body is not functioning in homeostasis, and biological function is impaired without evidence of damage, that should be known as a syndrome. In other words, you may spell the word syndrome, 's-i-n-d-r-o-m-e,' because sin is inhibiting proper bodily functions. Well, you know, I say that with 'tongue in cheek,' but behind a syndrome are thoughts and actions that are not of God—sin. A thought can trigger the body to not serve the person properly, but go into disorder or 'dis-ease' of function. When a body goes into 'dis-ease', there is a lack of ease or peace, and that makes the body feel like it is 'out of whack.' That ungodly thought is causing an imbalance of homeostasis producing a malfunction.

The manifestation of a 'sin-drome' or syndrome comes in two ways. The first is genetic. Earlier I explained genetic code defect behind bipolar/manic depression, but there is another dimension left undetected unless you know your enemy. Science does not understand this; the church is barely understanding it. They are called 'familial spirits.' What is a familial spirit? These are not 'familiar' spirits. Those

Chapter 3

would be operating in divination such as can be found in the incident between King Saul and the witch of Endor, who had a familiar spirit. In contrast, a familial spirit is an evil spirit, characterized and known by its fallen nature, that tracks specific family trees. If you go over to Deuteronomy 5:9-10, it refers to 'iniquities'; it does not say sins, folks. From the context of this scripture, iniquity is defined as generational sin. Generational sins visit multiple generations through temptation and thought patterns that replicate themselves from one generation to the next for three to four generations. They manifest as weaknesses in character and conduct that follow family trees. Verse 9 says, "The iniquities of the fathers shall be visited to the third and fourth generation of them that hate me." Verse 10 says, "But to them, that love me and keep my commandments mercy to thousands." In context, it is referring to thousand of generations of descendants.

> **⁹ Thou shalt not bow down thyself unto them, nor serve them: for I the LORD thy God *am* a jealous God, visiting the iniquity of the fathers upon the children unto the third and fourth *generation* of them that hate me, ¹⁰ And shewing mercy unto thousands of them that love me and keep my commandments.**　　　　　　　　　　Deuteronomy 5:9-10

We have not even been here that long since Adam. It has been thousands of years. Observe carefully what the scriptures say, "The iniquities of the fathers shall be visited." 'Visited' does not mean automatically passed down to the next generation. It means temptation will come to members of a family tree ,and if they yield to those thoughts they will reap the consequences. If they agree with the enemy, it will produce the same syndromes and diseases from the previous generation, because they embraced a way of thinking that is not of God. So the enemy is training a family how to become diseased. Are you tracking with me? We are ignorant of this process, yet it is easily understood in Scripture and also exhibited through science. Familial spirits influence our thoughts producing aberrations of biological function through what is known as the 'mind-body connection.' Instead, based upon our understanding, we call it the 'spirit-soul-body connection,' because it involves the third part of you. The third part of you is your spirit.

A genetic defect may lie latent as if it is sleeping until a life circumstance,

The Connection Between Relationships & Depression

especially involving conflict with others, real or perceived causes it to manifest. A conflict does not need to be real but simply based upon perception. A lot of people believe others do not like them without evidence. It is not because of any words spoken or any actions committed, but it is based upon a feeling that the other party does not like them. It is not even real; it is just perceived. However, this hypothetical thought will trigger the genetic defect to manifest and produce a biological change resulting in a disease or syndrome.

One example is a condition resulting in neuropathy of the spine. The condition is called Marie-Charcot-Tooth disease. Marie-Charcot-Tooth disease is named after the three doctors that discovered this syndrome: Doctor Marie, Doctor Charcot, and Doctor Tooth. Neuropathy of the spine is a condition that produces a dying off of nerve endings at a certain part of the spine responsible for motor control. This condition results in a stiffening of muscles in the back part of the leg and also causes a curvature of the instep or a bowing producing a limp. Marie-Charcot-Tooth disease is actually a syndrome, because there is nothing biologically wrong causing the nerve endings to die. When we deal with peripheral neuropathy the nerve endings die and the extremities have no feeling. Anytime a person's nerve endings begin to die, this type of profile of disease has one common spiritual problem. They do not like themselves. They struggle with self-accusation and self-hatred.

If you put your body down and put yourself down, your body will start to disintegrate. You must love yourself. I do not mean you should be stuck on yourself in conceit and arrogance. However, you must accept yourself and stop 'picking' at your flaws and weaknesses. If you do not accept yourself, your body will begin to decay, because you set in motion the principles of death instead of life. God has accepted you and He is life.

> **For in him we live, and move, and have our being; as certain also of your own poets have said, For we are also his offspring.** Acts 17:28

> **I call heaven and earth to record this day against you, *that* I have set before you life and death, blessing and cursing: therefore choose life, that both thou and thy seed may live:**
> Deuteronomy 30:19

Chapter 3

If Father God, who has accepted you, is life then He will sustain your life in your generation. But if you put yourself down and agree with spirits of self-accusation and self-hatred, you are removing yourself from God's sustaining power of life. You are releasing the spirit of death and infirmity to destroy you to convince you that you are right that you are no good, and you need to die and move on. By what you believe, you set in motion biological functions. Be careful! There is one kingdom wanting to bless you and the other wants to 'bless you' with the opposite of God's blessings. All disease is the blessing of Satan that comes on people who would rather believe a lie, his way of thinking, rather than believe the truth.

> **[10] And with all deceivableness of unrighteousness in them that perish; because they received not the love of the truth, that they might be saved. [11] And for this cause God shall send them strong delusion, that they should believe a lie:**   2 Thessalonians 2:10-11

I am telling you point blank it is that simple. In the generations, this phenomenon continues to occur. I believe we need to do some damage control, get back and start teaching God's people how to live a victorious life and not in superstition!

We need to be able to teach principles of life and living; that God will honor. I was teaching a conference in British Columbia years ago. It was the day of ministry, and I was teaching people how to pray for others. I was 'coaching' them on how to minister at a large conference of almost 800 people. One of those ministering came to me and said, "There's a young lady that we're praying for that has been diagnosed with Marie-Charcot-Tooth disease." Well, I did not know of it, and I had not a heard tell of it. But I usually carry some medical manuals, a Merck manual, and other things so I can investigate people's weird conditions. So I said, "Give me some time so I can look this thing up." So I looked up Marie-Charcot-Tooth disease in the Merck manual, and I found something very fascinating. It is a genetic defect. It is in the gene present at birth. The gene that produces this syndrome will lay latent. This neuropathy of the spine can manifest in any decade of that person's life from teens, 20's, 30's, 40's, 50's to 60's and beyond. It can happen in any decade, but usually will be released to manifest this neuropathy in conjunction with an emotional conflict.

Now, what connection is there between an emotional conflict and genetics? It is

The Connection Between Relationships & Depression

the same thing with viruses. Viruses can be activated by thought as well. So what is the connection between a virus and thought? The herpes virus can lay latent inside the person that has it until that person goes into a fear triggering conflict. Maybe it is a relationship breakdown, and they become fearful and all of a sudden they have a herpes outbreak. You know what causes a herpes outbreak? Anxiety. It is well known in psychiatric circles. That is what causes it. Now, what connection is there between a thought and a virus? What connection is there between a thought and a gene? When I read this, I wondered, "What kind of conflict did she have?" So I said, "God, this is a new one to me, help me think."

When they came back to see if I knew anything, I told them I did not. Then I thought and asked, "How old is she?" They responded, "She's about 35."

Then I had this incredible thought and said, "Go ask her, 'Did she fall in love with a young man that dumped her? Now, does she have grief because she blames herself and believes it was something in her that caused him not to like her?' If so, now she has self-hatred which would cause neuropathy. Go ask her."

They came back and said, "Well, you nailed that one. She began to cry. Yes, she fell love with a young man, and he dumped her, and within a year she developed the syndrome." I said, "You know what you have to do, don't you? You have to go back and help her forgive that young man. She's not guilty. In fact, she was saved from a real jerk. That was God's mercy, and you need to tell her that. God loved her so much that the devil got stirred up in that young man, because he didn't appreciate her as a gift and God saved her from a very dangerous, unhappy relationship." They ministered to her.

Dealing with a condition involving genetic defect poses the question, "Is it possible to change genetic defect through prayer?" Well, to begin with, that depends on if you believe in healing at all. If you believe in healing, it is important to have a Scriptural understanding of healing. In the gifts of the Holy Spirit, there are two: one is the gift of healing, and the other is the gift of miracles.

> [8] **For to one is given by the Spirit the word of wisdom; to another the word of knowledge by the same Spirit;** [9] **To another faith by the same Spirit; to another the gifts of healing by the same Spirit;** [10] **To another the working of miracles; to another prophecy; to another**

Chapter 3

> discerning of spirits; to another *divers* kinds of tongues; to another the interpretation of tongues: ¹¹ But all these worketh that one and the selfsame Spirit, dividing to every man severally as he will.
>
> 1 Corinthians 12:8-11

If we were to pray for bipolar and we were to repent for sin, cast out the evil spirits involved, and begin the journey out of the mindsets of depression, it would be essential to change the genetic code defect as well.

The gift of healing, as a work of the Holy Spirit, causes the bodily issue to cease and the body to heal. The gift of miracles is quite different. There are body parts that do not heal. That is why there are organ transplants. That is, also, why there is very little evidence of brain cell regeneration or nerve regeneration. In the gift of miracles listed in 1 Corinthians, it indicates it is for the believers of the current church age. Well, it is supposed to be, but it is not in operation very often. So how do you operate in the gift of miracles? In the gift of miracles, you call those things that are not as if they are in Jesus name. In faith, you are believing that God will re-form a body part that is either missing or impaired. You are expecting Father God, by His Spirit, to honor your words and a body part that does not naturally heal will be reformed out of nothing as if it were never damaged.

I am just a guy. I am just Henry. I am not a divine being. I have been trying to help God with His people for a long time. In forming body parts out of nothing, I have seen God honor my words a few times. Arms grow that needed to grow; body parts formed. I have seen stroke victims go from being hobbled and then healthy at the snap of a finger when God restored the brain cells over motor control that produced the stroke. I mention this not to promote what God has done through me, but I am writing so that you will read and have the faith to believe that healing and creative miracles are possible.

Additionally, if we are going to defeat bipolar, we are going to have to deal with generations of unloveliness. You are going to have to recognize that it is the product of not being loved, not feeling accepted, and being driven. It follows generations of men who did not know how to love and nurture their wives and their children. This is a classic example, folks. I have seen it time and time again. It is still here today. Do you think that every man knows how to love his wife and children in the Christian

The Connection Between Relationships & Depression

church, forget about the world? Often, they do not even know what day it is half the time. I am not making this point to denigrate any men reading this or to make them feel guilty or bad about themselves. I am one of you. I was not always a good father or a good husband either. So I do not have any stones to cast at anyone. Come on. We are all a bunch of 'fellas in a ship' working toward the same goal. We can defeat generational iniquity. We can defeat generationally inherited genetic disorders, and we can even defeat the forces that are coming to influence us as they have our families for generations.

Let me give you another example of familial spirits. This is about my son-in-law and my daughter. Pastor Scott is my son-in-law, and Sarah is my daughter. Scott was working with us in the ministry, and they just had Hannah, our granddaughter. One day Scott came to work looking like 'death warmed over' and bleary eyed. I thought he was going to fall asleep talking to me.

I said, "What happened?" He said, "Hannah kept us awake all night with colic." It was so bad that they put Hannah in a clothes basket on the dryer and turned it on hoping the shaking would put the child to sleep.

I responded, "Man, are you serious? You did that?" "Well, dad, we were desperate."

When children have colic, some misguided parents will pick the child up, shake it and yell to stop the screaming. The baby does not even understand English yet, and now the parents appear to be a monster. You think that child had fear before? Now it has it in bunches. That is absolute abuse.

Having heard about his situation, I responded, "Oh, colic, a piece of cake. She inherited your insecurity and fear. Colic is a result of a spirit of fear that is releasing a signal in the central nervous system of a baby who does not even know how to think yet. Inherited fear and insecurities are working in the central nervous system causing the intestine to twist producing the pain of colic. I said, "What you need to do is go home and cast out the spirits of insecurity and fear that were in you and that your daughter inherited. Command them to go in Jesus name, speak peace and freedom to your daughter then go to sleep."

He said, "You make that sound simple." I said, "Why complicate it?"

The next day Scott came to work smiling. He said, "Dad you won't believe this," he then corrected himself, "No, you'll believe it." I said, "Well, you're looking happy."

Chapter 3

He said, "Dad, we did what you said. Then we put Hannah to bed, and we went to bed and woke up the next morning and slept all night." She never had colic again. Scott and Sarah have had other children after Hannah. Hannah was the first of eight that he has had with Sarah, and none of them have had colic. This is how it should work. Would you agree with that?

Do you believe it is possible that we could speak to defective genes, if we are dealing with a life circumstance, and command those defective genes to be changed, so they do not result in a reduction of serotonin as a byproduct? That is what is happening. In the bipolar profile, genes are causing serotonin to be diminished in combination with thoughts and wrong spirituality. Are you tracking with me? I know this could seem complicated. Probably some of you are thinking, "What in the world? Where is this guy coming from and what is the meaning of this information?" Well, I believe this subject is important to examine especially because even the world does not know this. They do not have God. Why do most churches not know this? They have not been taught.

I have traveled amongst the Christian church for 30 years. I have not found many churches that even care about what I teach to help their people. But I have found that people within the 'flock' love it. So why are the people more hungry than their leaders? Folks, it is because there is a real dearth of God in the Christian church. We have a form of godliness, but we either deny the power of God or do not know how to apply the Word to bring about healing. Healing is supposed to be the children's bread.

> [25] **Then came she and worshipped him, saying, Lord, help me.** [26] **But he answered and said, It is not meet to take the children's bread, and to cast** *it* **to dogs.** [27] **And she said, Truth, Lord: yet the dogs eat of the crumbs which fall from their masters' table.** Matthew 15:25-27

If you do not believe that God heals today, then for you, He never will. If you think healing passed away with the apostles two thousand years ago and you can show it to me in Scripture, I will 'cut your cabbage for free for one million years.' In other words, there is no evidence it passed away, and there is plenty of evidence that God Is working today in the same way He did during Jesus' day. If you were to say,

The Connection Between Relationships & Depression

when I minister in Jesus name, that the healing of the sick and casting out devils is because I have a devil then you have committed the unpardonable sin. Be careful. Be very careful. If you have been taught and believed that healing has passed away, I strongly suggest you re-investigate the Scriptures for yourself rather than accepting the teachings of other men. Healing and creative miracles and casting out of evil spirits have not passed away. Believing that God will heal and remove evil from our lives is an important part of our faith. The Bible asks, "When the Son of Man returns shall he find faith in the earth?"

I tell you that he will avenge them speedily. Nevertheless when the Son of man cometh, shall he find faith on the earth? Luke 18:8

I do not mean to preach to you. However, the home and family must be a safe place of peace to prevent these disorders from manifesting. It seems from clinical observation that reduced levels of serotonin are found in bipolar cases. When a person does not feel safe, loved, or accepted their body responds by reducing the amount of serotonin causing depression. It is plausible that genetic defects are a result of family dynamics. This is particularly problematic in families where fathers do not conduct themselves in a manner providing acceptance and safety for their wives and children. I found this in just about every case history. I trust I have learned something over thirty years of experience helping people. This is not an indictment. If you went to a doctor to find out why you were sick, would you be offended if he told you the truth? Then please do not be offended if I tell you the truth. I love you, I care for you, and I am teaching you to defeat evil spirits and disease. It is my observation that serotonin is usually depleted in individuals that do not feel loved and accepted.

In the days of Nehemiah and Ezra, by the decree of Cyrus, the Israelites were released from captivity to go back to Jerusalem and Israel to rebuild the temple. Ezra began to read from the Law of God in Nehemiah chapter 8. He read to those coming out of captivity and it revealed why their parents went into captivity; why they had been there seventy years. It was because they disobeyed the Word of God. By rebelling against the Word, they had chosen captivity and curses. God had no

Chapter 3

choice, but to send them into a foreign land. They were taken there, because they did not want God and His ways. They were taken away captive to a country that did not love God. The Word of God was not there. But when they came back and they heard the reading of the Word in Nehemiah 9:2, it exposed the need for a change of heart.

> **And the seed of Israel separated themselves from all strangers, and stood and confessed their sins, and the iniquities of their fathers.** Nehemiah 9:2

Everybody wants to be prayed for, but do they want to follow God? You need to 'know the truth, and the truth shall make you free.' What I am teaching you is designed to give you the faith to believe. This is not blind faith but real faith, because you are using your faculties of understanding. The seed of Israel separated themselves from all strangers, and they stood and confessed their sins and the iniquities of their fathers. Is it possible we could defeat this familial issue producing genetic defect that is manifesting as bipolar? We need to come to Father God and say, "Father, in our generations we recognize we have had fathers that were not and did not know how to be husbands and fathers properly. It could have skipped a generation, but we see evidence that this could be why we have these problems. So we recognize that we may not be loving as we should, and we are not being that father or husband we should be. We take responsibility and repent to you, Father, and ask you to forgive us for our sins and to release us from the iniquities of our fathers. We ask that the power of this spirituality and mindset of the villain running in our generations may be broken that our seed may be blessed and not be carriers of these chromosomal defects in our family. We ask that our children and their children's children will never have bipolar again as long as they understand and apply the truth."

God will not force your children and families to follow the truth. You can teach your families if they want to listen. However, if they do not want to hear you, you cannot force them either. Well, now you know how God feels, because He's truth and sometimes nobody wants to listen. Are you willing to listen?

CHAPTER 4:
Choosing to Overcome Depression

Are you getting the picture of what is happening in your life? Because what I am teaching you covers all ranges of physical problems, not just depression. In fact, you make your health from within, and you make your disease from within. So do not be overtaken by a disorder or a disease like some strange thing happened to you. It is the byproduct of other decisions. I learned something from Deuteronomy chapter 28. In verses 1 and 2 it says, "It shall come to pass if you hear what God said, and you'll do what He said, then all these blessings shall come upon you and overtake you."

> **¹ And it shall come to pass, if thou shalt hearken diligently unto the voice of the Lord thy God, to observe and to do all his commandments which I command thee this day, that the Lord thy God will set thee on high above all nations of the earth: ² And all these blessings shall come on thee, and overtake thee, if thou shalt hearken unto the voice of the Lord thy God.**   Deuteronomy 28:1-2

When I went down through the 12 verses following verses 1 and 2, there was not one disease listed in all the blessings. So I came to a conclusion that to not have a disease was a blessing and that to have a disorder or disease is not a blessing. That is still where I am in the conclusion of the matter.

Now, the reasons for disorders or diseases are interesting. I want to take you to a few case histories and show you a few principles. The beginning of our problem began with Adam and Eve. The Bible says, "Through one man's disobedience, sin entered into the world and death by sin."

Chapter 4

Wherefore, as by one man sin entered into the world, and death by sin; and so death passed upon all men, for that all have sinned: Romans 5:12

'Through one man's disobedience…' If you look through the story of Adam and Eve in Genesis 3:1-13, you will find that they disobeyed God's Word. Eve disobeyed, and then Adam did nothing to cover his wife. He agreed with her, disobeyed, and that opened the door to evil. I love this story, because it shows us this invisible kingdom that influences our thoughts and actions. I believe you will identify with their battleground as we investigate this historic event.

The serpent spoke to Eve and questioned God's Word and began to add and take away from it. The serpent said, "If you eat of this fruit and disobey God's Word you shall not die." That is right in verse 4. It says, "For God knows that in the day that you eat this fruit your eyes will be open and you shall be as gods." In the Hebrew language, the word 'gods' refers to lowercase 'g' gods or spirit beings, instead of uppercase 'G' God. This scripture is actually referring to devils. In other words, this scripture is saying, "you shall be as us, devils, knowing good and evil."

4 And the serpent said unto the woman, Ye shall not surely die: 5 For God doth know that in the day ye eat thereof, then your eyes shall be opened, and ye shall be as gods, knowing good and evil.   Genesis 3:4-5

Before eating of the fruit, Adam and Eve were immune to evil and what it represented. There was a barrier to their spirits. When they disobeyed God's Word, by their actions, they embraced the word of the enemy. That enemy's word became truth to them and God's Word became a lie to them. They followed the enemy's lie and not the truth of the Word. This leads to verse 7: "And the eyes of them both were open, and they knew they were naked."

And the eyes of them both were opened, and they knew that they *were* naked; and they sewed fig leaves together, and made themselves aprons.   Genesis 3:7

They were naked before they realized they were naked. However, when their eyes were opened, and they saw their nakedness, it was a shame to them. Adam and

CHOOSING TO OVERCOME DEPRESSION

Eve were about to go into a depressed state. This is a classic case of depression. They did not know what was going on. But, the first thing that came to them was shame. Then in verse 8 when they heard the voice of the Lord they went into fear and guilt.

> **And they heard the voice of the LORD God walking in the garden in the cool of the day: and Adam and his wife hid themselves from the presence of the LORD God amongst the trees of the garden.**
> Genesis 3:8

Then in verses 9-13 we have fear and accusation. Both Adam and Eve were filled with accusation. They hid from God in fear and then accused each other and the serpent for their actions. They had fear, guilt, and shame. Their reaction to hearing the voice of the Lord after eating of the fruit marks a significant turning point. The Lord would come and walk with them in the cool of the evening in the garden of Eden, as was His custom. He came, after their eyes were opened, and they saw that they were naked. They made the first bikinis and hid. This was because they had fear, guilt, and shame. The Lord came looking for them, and they were not in the pathway for the evening walk. The Lord began to call out for them wanting to know where they were. "Where are you?" Finally, Adam had enough courage; I suppose because he responded. When the Lord said, "Adam where are you?" He said, "Here I am Lord." "Uh, where are you, Adam?" "Out here in the bushes, Lord." "And why are you out here in the bushes, Adam?" "Hiding from you, Lord." "Why are you hiding from me, Adam?" "Because, Lord, we are naked."

> **⁹ And the LORD God called unto Adam, and said unto him, Where *art* thou? ¹⁰ And he said, I heard thy voice in the garden, and I was afraid, because I *was* naked; and I hid myself.**
> Genesis 3:9-10

The Lord did not tell Adam he had a psychosis. He did not say to Adam, "You have a psychiatric problem, son." He did not say to Adam, "You need a little inner healing or counseling." He did not say to Adam, "Listen, you have a chemistry imbalance. You're a little depressed, so I'm going to get you a little sassafras root and mix it

Chapter 4

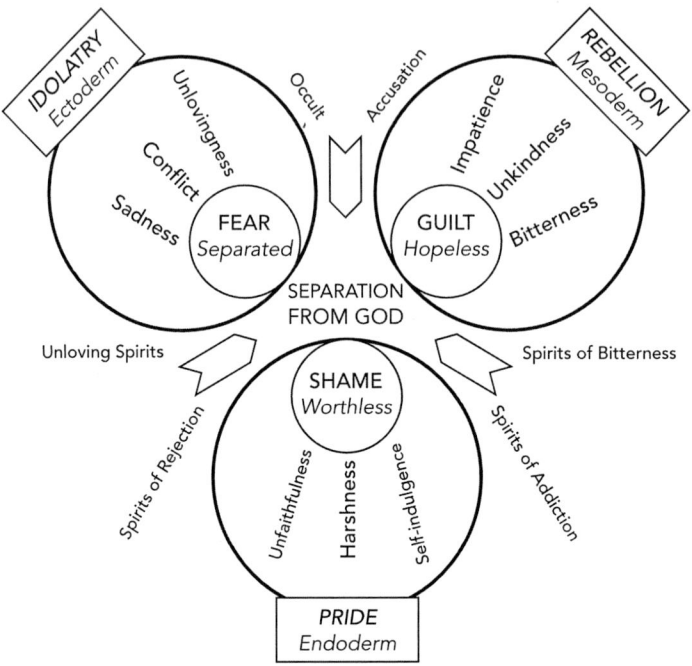

Diagram 3: Separation from God chart showing the fear, shame and guilt that came into Adam and Eve in the garden. The fruit of sin manifests through other spiritual issues. Endoderm, Ectoderm and Mesoderm of our

with this other ingredient and make a potion and give you an antidepressant." Listen carefully to what the Lord said to Adam, "Who told you, you were naked?"

> **And he said, Who told thee that thou *wast* naked? Hast thou eaten of the tree, whereof I commanded thee that thou shouldest not eat?** Genesis 3:11

'Who told you that you were naked?' Adam and Eve had thoughts that they had not learned. They had emotions and feelings that they had not been taught. They were flooded with feelings and emotions and thoughts that were not of God. They went into a phobic depressed state and ran and hid. When the Lord coaxed them out of the bushes, they turned on Him and against each other.

> **[12] And the man said, The woman whom thou gavest *to be* with me, she gave me of the tree, and I did eat. [13] And the LORD God said unto the woman, What *is* this *that* thou hast done? And the woman said, The serpent beguiled me, and I did eat.** Genesis 3:12-13

CHOOSING TO OVERCOME DEPRESSION

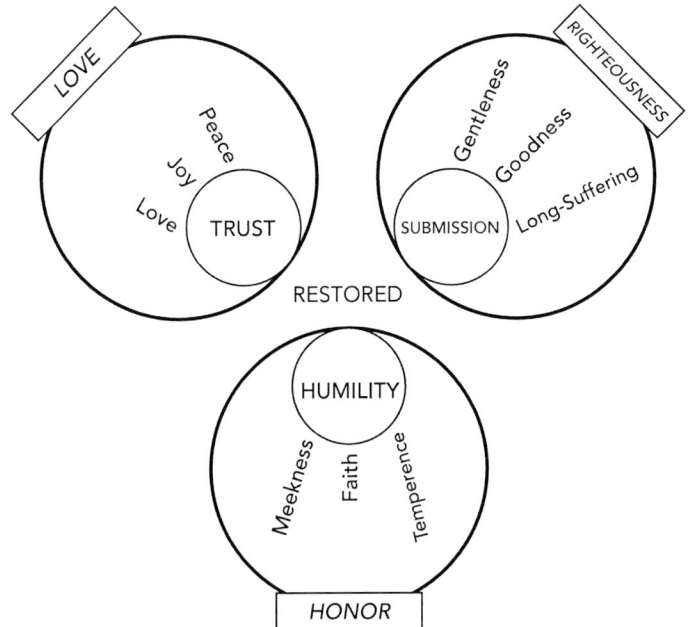

Diagram 4: Restored to God chart shows the three areas of our life functioning as God intended. This is what was lost in the garden of Eden. Apart from sin, this is what we should look like including the fruit, manifested through how we think, speak and act as we are restored to the Godhead.

Their response was psychotic. So you have psychosis, you have depression, you have fear, you have guilt, you have shame. All of this came in at one time. That is how quickly it came. What came into them is still here today. It is in every church in the world. It is in every city and every nation. They became fearful and separated from God. They became separated from their creator. They became separated from their friend who would walk with them in the cool of the evening. Why would you be afraid of someone that was your friend? Accusation. This is separation from God. They had feelings of being unloved. They had conflict, and sadness. They were getting all goofed up. In fact, what you see here coming out of the fall of Adam and Eve is the profile of all psychiatric diseases. All of it is displayed in diagram 3.

The foundation for it is all here. It is also the foundation for most biological disease. All of it is right here. You may recognize some of these sins in your life. Well, flush it. Get rid of it. Why are you feeding on something that is not good for you? You do not eat rotten food. Why do you eat bad spiritual food? Why do you accept things that are not good for you in the spiritual when you do not accept things that are not

Chapter 4

good for you in the natural? Why do you accept things that are bad for you spiritually and psychologically as if they were normal? It is abnormal. Everything you see in this diagram is abnormal to God. Not only did they become separated from God, but they also became separated from themselves. They began to have guilt, bitterness, unkindness, impatience and rebellion. There was a little accusation in there because Adam accused his wife. They accused God in the process, and they accused the serpent. They decided they needed a scapegoat rather than take ownership for their actions. There is no indication that Adam and Eve ever repented to the Lord. Not one scripture validates that position.

They became separated from others. They felt worthless. They had shame, because they felt like they did not measured up. They had unfaithfulness and self-indulgence, pride, guilt, and were separated from God. They felt hopeless about themselves and worthless in the face of others. You can see bits and pieces of this in those around us today. Occasionally, one or two of these things manifest in your life. So I do not mean to oppress you with this 'X-Ray vision' inspection of your spirituality, but this is the foundation for depression and all disease. Our lives could change if we came before God allowed him to change us and get our minds and our spirituality straightened out. If we stop acting like other goofy people and decide to be normal, as far as God is concerned, we might look like the next chart. You might end up looking like this:

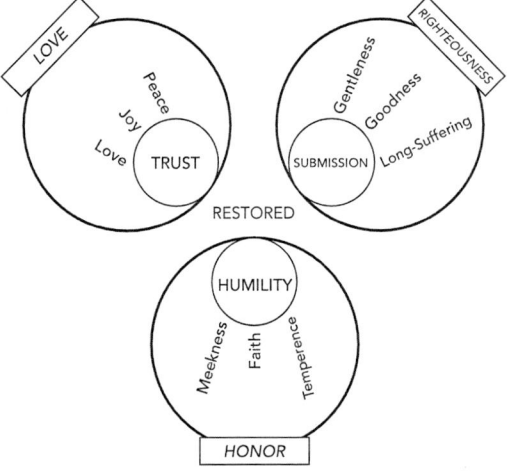

This is what was lost in the garden. Through Jesus Christ, Father God has been recovering what He lost in the tragedy of the garden of Eden. That is the power of the cross. The Father is re-capturing and recovering what he lost. You are a product of that recovery and restoration. You are being called out of darkness and being transformed. But you cannot be transformed unless you are informed by the Word. You cannot be

CHOOSING TO OVERCOME DEPRESSION

transformed because 'faith comes by hearing, and hearing by the Word of God.'

So then faith *cometh* by hearing, and hearing by the word of God. Romans 10:17

So this is not by some kind of instinct. The kingdom of God does not run by instinct; it runs by the Word. The spoken Word of God and the written Word of God replaces instinct. Animals have instinct, and you are not an animal. You are a spiritual being. So let us not act like the animal kingdom any longer.

Would it not be wonderful to be the kind of person in the second diagram? Looking at these attributes, you could say, "Hey, I look pretty good, don't I?" If this is part of the fabric of your personality and your spirituality, disease and depression cannot touch you. There is no room for it. There is no room for it, because love covers a multitude of sins.

And above all things have fervent charity among yourselves: for charity shall cover the multitude of sins. 1 Peter 4:8

How can you be upset with somebody that is peaceable? How can you be upset with somebody that is full of love and joy? This is supposed to be your character and nature. It is called the fruit of the Holy Spirit. In Galatians, this is not the work of the Holy Spirit for God. It is the work of the Holy Spirit for you, as the sons and daughters of God.

[22] But the fruit of the Spirit is love, joy, peace, longsuffering, gentleness, goodness, faith,
[23] Meekness, temperance: against such there is no law. Galatians 5:22-23

The fruit the Holy Spirit wants to produce the fruit of His work with you. If you allow the Holy Spirit to convict you and deal with you, by the will of the Father in Jesus' name, He will form God's nature in you.

I love what it says in Galatians 5. If you allow God to reform your nature back to what He intended the Bible says, "Against such, there is no law."

Meekness, temperance: against such there is no law. Galatians 5:23

Chapter 4

How would you like to be immune to psychiatric and biological disease? You may say, "That's utopian." No, that is the gospel. God is not responsible for the failure of men; men and the devil are. We need to get back on the right team and follow God and not the devil. Stop working for the wrong 'father' and get back on the right side of the family tree. Welcome to the family business. The family business of taking back this planet for Father God as He intended.

'Against such, there is no law.' Wow, that is powerful. Trusting God, feeling in right standing with God, not having to jockey for superiority, being humble in your position, and relaxing and enjoying freedom are all the benefits your true Father will provide. One of the great promises of the Millennium, when Christ returns, is the indication that natural people will embrace the nature of God under our rulership, as kings and priest. They will have the freedom to go from house to house breaking bread and having fellowship one with another. No more barred windows. No more gates of steel and barbed wire. They will live in safety with no fear of each other. Lord have mercy, I am ready for this to happen now.

But you may say, "It's not happening now." Why not? Do you think who you are is dependent on what other people are doing or saying? What I do is not dependent on what anybody else does at all. I do not let other people be my standard of righteousness. I do not have other people decide my spirituality. I am not interested in playing the revenge game or the blame game, or the name game, or the accusation game or the slander game. I am not interested. I am too busy helping people. I am so busy helping people I do not have time to hurt them. So if people are so busy hurting people, it is probably because they are not trying to help anybody. If you are trying to help somebody, you will not hurt them.

Section 1
God's Code for Life

I am going to take you to Luke 10. I want to show you a couple of scriptures. I call Luke 10:25-28, *'God's Code for Life.'* We should be living by God's Code for Life. The scripture begins, "Behold a certain lawyer stood up and tempted him saying, 'Master, what shall I do to inherit eternal life?' And Jesus said unto him, 'What is written in the law?' And he answered and said, 'You shall love the Lord your God with all your heart,

Choosing to Overcome Depression

and with all your soul, and with all your strength and with all your mind, and love your neighbor as yourself.' And Jesus said unto him, 'You have answered right, this do, and you shall live.'"

> [25] And, behold, a certain lawyer stood up, and tempted him, saying, Master, what shall I do to inherit eternal life? [26] He said unto him, What is written in the law? how readest thou? [27] And he answering said, Thou shalt love the Lord thy God with all thy heart, and with all thy soul, and with all thy strength, and with all thy mind; and thy neighbour as thyself. [28] And he said unto him, Thou hast answered right: this do, and thou shalt live.
>
> Luke 10:25-28

Folks, this is supposed to be a secret. We are always looking for some magic bullet to guarantee us something. This is the narrow gate right here, folks. The church needs to stop what they are doing, read this, embrace it and teach nothing else until everybody has got it. It is the key to life. I am a life coach right now. I want you to win this.

You may say, "I don't feel like it." Who asked you to go by your feelings? I do not follow my feelings. If I had followed my feelings, I would have problems. If I followed every temptation of the devil, Lord, have mercy. Temptation comes just like a wind all the time to all of you, right? So how do we deal with this?

You may have the thought, "Well, I don't want to be tempted." Instead, we should embrace it. It is the trying of your faith. It reveals who you are. You have to have a spine. You have to have a spine and choose to make quality decisions. I decide to forgive. I do not even have to think about it. Well, in the past, I had to think about it as I was learning to apply the Word. Today, when people speak evil of me, and they often do through websites and people here and there, I choose to forgive. They stoned the prophets. So I am in pretty good company when I am accused. I no longer have to go to my closet and pull out my forgiveness coat. I am always wearing it. It is part of my nature. I am a forgiving person. I do not hold a record of wrongs. I love my enemies. I miss people that hate me. I miss them. I was talking to my wife, Pastor Donna, the other day. I said, "Some of those loose cannons that used to come through here. I miss those loose cannons." I do not miss the noise they made, but

Chapter 4

you have to give your heart to somebody. Love does not change, because of the failure of another to meet it and reciprocate with love. Let me repeat it. I said, "Love does not change, because of the failure of another to meet it." God's love has not changed even with the rejection of the world to the gospel message. He is constant.

You may rebut, "Yeah, but I feel their rejection." So, what are you going to do with that feeling?

There is no way to prevent you and me from being pierced by the evil in others, but you do not have to internalize it. When you are 'wounded' and you say, "Well, I'm wounded." Then you are indicating that you are keeping a record of wrongs, because love does not even pay attention when wrong is done to it. It does not have a record of wrongs. It believes all things, bears all things.

> **4 Charity suffereth long, *and* is kind; charity envieth not; charity vaunteth not itself, is not puffed up, 5 Doth not behave itself unseemly, seeketh not her own, is not easily provoked, thinketh no evil; 6 Rejoiceth not in iniquity, but rejoiceth in the truth; 7 Beareth all things, believeth all things, hopeth all things, endureth all things.** 1 Corinthians 13:4-7

Your love should not be based on the reciprocation of another person. Just be love. If I was with someone else walking down the street tomorrow and I recognized you I would like to be able to say, "Hey, there goes Love. Hey, Love! How are you doing today, Love?" Or could I also say, "How are you doing today, Faith? How are you doing, Long-suffering?" I am passionate about this subject because I want you to understand and be able to defeat depression. However, what I am teaching you is not just about depression. All types of disease can be defeated on the same basis; whether it is psychiatric, psychological, biological, or spiritual. Folks, the principles of the kingdom of God work in all three dimensions. Quit looking at yourself from the outside and what you look like and how you sound. Look at yourself from the inside out. Quit judging people on the outside. Reverse the process. What did Jesus say? "You've answered right, this do, and you shall live." Do what? Love the Lord your God with all of your heart (spirit man), all of your soul (psych, psychology, mind) and with all of your strength (physiological). That encompasses spirit, soul, and body. And love your neighbor as you love yourself.

CHOOSING TO OVERCOME DEPRESSION

And the second *is* like unto it, Thou shalt love thy neighbour as thyself. Matthew 22:39

You cannot love your neighbor if you do not love yourself. You are a fabricated personality–smokiness, pretentious, hiding the pain of not feeling loved by performance and pretending everything is fine. You cannot love yourself if you have not received the love of God your Father. It is not possible.

So would you make peace with your Father again? Choose to make peace with yourself about yourself. Then you will be able to have peace with others. The reason you do not have peace with others is that you do not have peace with yourself. The reason you do not have peace with yourself is that you do not have peace with God. You are still hedging your bets that God does not love you. The enemy wants to make you feel that He does not. In Matthew 22:37-40, Jesus quotes the same theme I just quoted, but then he said, "Upon this, love the Lord your God, love your neighbor as yourself hang all of the law and the prophets."

[37] Jesus said unto him, Thou shalt love the Lord thy God with all thy heart, and with all thy soul, and with all thy mind. [38] This is the first and great commandment. [39] And the second *is* like unto it, Thou shalt love thy neighbour as thyself. [40] On these two commandments hang all the law and the prophets. Matthew 22:37-40

The foundation of the gospel, Old Testament and New, is relationship. From what we have observed, 80% of all disorders and diseases including depression are the result of separation on three levels. The first is separation from the Godhead; the Father, the Word, and the Holy Spirit. The second is you being separated from yourself about yourself. The third is you being separated from others. The beginning of all healing and the beginning of all prevention of disorders and diseases is being reconciled to the Godhead, being reconciled to yourself about yourself and being prepared to be reconciled to others in your heart regardless of what they do. That is the beginning of your life. Do you want life? Jesus gave you the secret. Not just for your present life, but your eternal life. You do not have to wait for eternity to find life. It is here now. You do not have to die of a disease. You do not have to be oppressed in your soul. You do not have to put up with it. But you have to know who to blame.

Chapter 4

You have been blaming the wrong parties. You have been blaming others, and blaming yourself, and blaming God. Meanwhile, the real enemy and his kingdom are laughing their heads off at your deception. They are the ones that gave you bad thoughts and then blamed you for them. They are the ones that put thoughts in your consciousness and then blame you because you have these same thoughts. Because you do not know what to do with it, you end up blaming God, yourself, and others. You have not entered into life. You are walking in death.

I do not mean to startle you or oppress you. I want you to live. I am not teaching to give you a fairy-tale or a nursery rhyme. You are reading to defeat something. I hope I leave you with enough tools to take ownership of your lives again regardless of how you feel. If you embrace the kingdom of God and the Word of God, the Spirit of God will work with you, and those feelings that accuse you will dissipate. They will be gone. As a result, you will be able to think and speak with clarity. The shadowy force of Satan's kingdom will not be there to occlude your thinking.

After Adam and Eve had disobeyed God, it did not take long for sin to become a larger and larger problem starting with their son, Cain. The iniquity of the father began to move through the generations. In the story of Cain and Abel, the Lord had favor towards Abel's sacrifice and not Cain's. Cain copped an attitude. In Genesis 4:5 it says, "Cain was wroth, and his countenance fell."

> **But unto Cain and to his offering he had not respect. And Cain was very wroth, and his countenance fell.**   Genesis 4:5

Do you know what that is? Have you ever seen a kid pout, because they felt rejected? They look like a gorilla hunched over with their arms hanging down. In verse 6, The Lord asked Cain, "Why are you angry and why has your countenance fallen? Why the long face?" Then the Lord asked Cain, "If you do well, shall you not be accepted?"

> **If thou doest well, shalt thou not be accepted? and if thou doest not well, sin lieth at the door. And unto thee *shall be* his desire, and thou shalt rule over him.**   Genesis 4:7

Choosing to Overcome Depression

In fact, the Lord said to Cain, "What is your problem? You're the eldest brother. Abel will serve you all the days of your life. You shall rule him because you're the eldest brother. What is your problem?"

And unto thee *shall be* his desire, and thou shalt rule over him.   Genesis 4:7c

And then the Lord said to Cain, "If you do well, will you not be accepted? And if you do not well, (read carefully) sin lieth at the door."

and if thou doest not well, sin lieth at the door.   Genesis 4:7b

That word 'lieth' is Hebrew 7257 in the Strong's Concordance. It means to crouch or to lurk. So the scripture may read, "And if you do not well, sin is crouching or lurking at your door..." To do what? Influence your thinking. To influence your thoughts and your emotions. Did Cain take the warning? No, he followed his feelings and his emotions. He developed hatred and bitterness, and in the field he killed his brother. He murdered Abel because he did not take the warning.

Are you taking the warning? Sin is lying and lurking at your door trying to destroy you, but it must have your permission to do so. You must embrace the thought for it to have power in your life. A sin is not reckoned a sin to you unless it works through your actions and words to fulfill itself. Before you choose to act on sin, it is temptation to you. I have a great teaching resource available on this subject, and it is called *7 Steps to Sin*. It will help you in your process of being an overcomer. When is sin reckoned to you as an action and when is it just temptation? It will help you to understand this subject in depth.

In the case of Adam and Eve, the question God posed was 'Who told you that you were naked?' In the case of Cain, the core issue was identifying the source of thoughts that did not originate in his mind, and resisting them. Satan's invisible kingdom was able to influence them from within. Jesus said this, "It's not what goes in the mouth and comes out 'Charmin-land' (the toilet) that defiles the man. It is that thing which comes from within, out of the heart of man, that defiles the man. From within proceed evil thoughts." It is from within not without. 'From within these things manifest and defile the man.'

Chapter 4

And he said, That which cometh out of the man, that defileth the man.　　　Mark 7:20

Did we not understand fundamental truth? 'From within' the other kingdom was there to influence them, to give them thoughts, feelings, and emotions, which they embraced and acted on as if it were their own minds, their own personalities, their own thoughts. You are so easily influenced by that kingdom. I hope you wake up, in this teaching, and do an inventory of all your thoughts, emotions, feelings, and impressions, and question the real source of these problems. Sometimes you need to pause and take a moment before you act on a thought and question its source. One simple way of pausing is counting to 10. Because if you do not pause and count to 10, you may be used by the enemy to cause some trouble by acting out any random thought or feeling. If I can get Christians to count to 10, they might hear the Holy Spirit. But sometimes people I deal with, do not pause to give the Holy Spirit a chance to speak to them. The distance between their brain and their tongue is zero, and they let whatever they think or feel manifest.

The next example of someone who did not discern the source of their thoughts was Judas. In Luke 22:3, Satan entered into Judas.

Then entered Satan into Judas surnamed Iscariot, being of the number of the twelve.

Luke 22:3

What that means is that Satan was able to access Judas' spirit and give him thoughts that took him to betraying the Lord. Judas did not have an original thought. He was a puppet on a string. Cain did not have an original thought. He was a puppet on a string. You may be a puppet on a string manipulated by the enemy. The enemy may be using you without you seeing that you are being used. That is why the Bible says, "Be not ignorant of Satan's devices and his methods." You may say, "I don't like thinking about Satan and evil spirits." I did not ask you to think about them. I asked you to be aware of them. Discerning of spirits is one of the nine gifts of the Holy Spirit.

CHOOSING TO OVERCOME DEPRESSION

> To another the working of miracles; to another prophecy; to another discerning of spirits; to another *divers* kinds of tongues; to another the interpretation of tongues:
> 1 Corinthians 12:10

Did you know that? I guess there must be something that needs to be discerned called an evil spirit. Discerning of spirits; if you discern them, do you invite them for breakfast, lunch, and dinner or do you remove them? When they come to you, you may say, "Get out of here! I don't want to listen to you anymore." Tell it to go. It does not read your mind. If you have a spirit of fear or anger or hatred or bitterness or lust or whatever, talk to it. It does not read your mind. "Listen to my voice; there is no vacancy. Get out of here." 'Resist the devil, and he shall flee.' But the church is passive. It goes into wishful thinking. When I see someone stuck, I will ask, "What are you doing?" They might respond, "Wishing the devil would go away and quit talking to me." It cannot read your mind; it does not hear you at all. It just sees you squinting your face concentrating on something.

One time an evil spirit came to bug me about ten years after it had been defeated in my life. It came to see if my house was filled or empty. It had been giving me thoughts and pictures of things that I thought I had defeated. The truth is that I had defeated it. But it came back as the scriptures say, "To see if I was filled or empty."

> [43] When the unclean spirit is gone out of a man, he walketh through dry places, seeking rest, and findeth none. [44] Then he saith, I will return into my house from whence I came out; and when he is come, he findeth *it* empty, swept, and garnished.
> Matthew 12:43-44

So I played possum and acted like I did not hear it or see it. It kept giving me more pictures, and more thoughts and kicked up the ante trying to lure me. It did not know if I was listening or not, because I gave no indication I was listening. I did not respond to it, but after a half hour, I just kind of got bored of it. And I said, "Boo!" I did not even say, "In the name of Jesus," and it was gone. It never came back again. I just said, "Boo!" I would not suggest you do that as part of your spiritual warfare, but it worked for me. It revealed that they cannot hear your thoughts. They are attempting to trap you in their thinking and convince you to agree with them.

Chapter 4

Case History Number Four: Peter, Simon Peter. The Lord said, "Simon, Simon, behold Satan hath desired to have you that he may sift you as wheat, but I have prayed for you that your faith fail not and when you are converted strengthen the brethren."

> **31 And the Lord said, Simon, Simon, behold, Satan hath desired *to have* you, that he may sift *you* as wheat: 32 But I have prayed for thee, that thy faith fail not: and when thou art converted, strengthen thy brethren.** Luke 22:31-32

Jesus did nothing to stop the sifting of Peter. He did nothing to stop the voice of Satan that would come to influence Peter. And Peter yielded, and he did everything the Lord said he would. He said, "Lord, I wouldn't do that," but he did it. He betrayed Jesus, he cursed, he went and did everything Jesus predicted. However, I submit to you that Peter's thoughts were not from his own mind. He was influenced by Satan, and he bought it, and he acted it out. But did he recover himself? Yes.

Moses is another classic case of depression. Numbers 11:1-23 is an example of a leader with depression. I will just give you the synopsis. The people of Israel were complaining. They were irritated and said, "Where's the beef? Where's the beef? We're tired of baklava (manna)." I like phrasing it that way. They were complaining. Moses went down under it. He was overwhelmed and in verses 10-15, he said to the Lord, "I am not able to bear all these people alone because it's too heavy for me and if you deal thus with me, Lord, kill me, I pray you, out of hand, if I found favor in your sight; and let me not see my wretchedness."

> **10 Then Moses heard the people weep throughout their families, every man in the door of his tent: and the anger of the LORD was kindled greatly; Moses also was displeased. 11 And Moses said unto the LORD, Wherefore hast thou afflicted thy servant? and wherefore have I not found favour in thy sight, that thou layest the burden of all this people upon me? 12 Have I conceived all this people? have I begotten them, that thou shouldest say unto me, Carry them in thy bosom, as a nursing father beareth the sucking child, unto the land which thou swarest unto their fathers? 13 Whence should I have flesh to give unto all this people? for they weep unto me, saying, Give us flesh, that we may eat. 14 I am not able to**

CHOOSING TO OVERCOME DEPRESSION

bear all this people alone, because *it is* too heavy for me. ⁱ⁵ And if thou deal thus with me, kill me, I pray thee, out of hand, if I have found favour in thy sight; and let me not see my wretchedness. Numbers 11:10-15

Do you know what Moses asked the Lord do? Kill him. I think he had a little depression, and he was somewhat suicidal, but he wanted to let the Lord do it. That way he could blame the Lord. But the Lord did not kill him. He had another plan. The plan included seventy elders that the Spirit of God would release to help Moses bear the burden of the people.

¹⁶ And the LORD said unto Moses, Gather unto me seventy men of the elders of Israel, whom thou knowest to be the elders of the people, and officers over them; and bring them unto the tabernacle of the congregation, that they may stand there with thee. ¹⁷ And I will come down and talk with thee there: and I will take of the spirit which *is* upon thee, and will put *it* upon them; and they shall bear the burden of the people with thee, that thou bear *it* not thyself alone. Numbers 11:16-17

Sometimes depression works because you are isolated. Maybe you are overwhelmed. Depression will take you away from people when you really need them most, because they can help you think things through. They can pray for you, they can love you, and they can encourage you to bring you out a dark place. Depression will prevent you from finding others to help you bear your burden. It will isolate you in a place where you believe no one cares for you, no one loves you, and that is the way it goes.

David is another example. In a story about David and the Philistines, the Israelites had their wives and children with them on a campaign, and when they went back to the camp, the Philistines had taken all them. This included David's wives and children along with all the men's wives and children. Then David and the people that were with him lifted up their voices and wept until they had no more power to weep. They were in distress. Verse 6 says, "And David was greatly distressed for the people spake of stoning him."

Chapter 4

And David was greatly distressed; for the people spake of stoning him, because the soul of all the people was grieved, every man for his sons and for his daughters: but David encouraged himself in the LORD his God. 1 Samuel 30:6

That is enough to cause you to be depressed. 'Because of the soul of the people were grieved, every man for his sons and his daughters. But David encouraged himself in the Lord.'

because the soul of all the people was grieved, every man for his sons and for his daughters: but David encouraged himself in the LORD his God. 1 Samuel 30:6b

In that state of grief for the despair of the moment he encouraged himself in the Lord. Then he had a thought—a God thought. You know sometimes in the middle of your darkness if you will begin to encourage yourself in the Lord, you may have a God thought to help you out of your mess. David did. He thought, "Go get the women and children." And they got them by defeating the Philistines. They saved all the wives and children back to safety and that is the end of that story.

Parkinson's Disease

Changing directions, I want to address serotonin deficiency and dopamine. This concerns the over and under secretion of dopamine, serotonin, and norepinephrine. Let me give you examples. On one side, there is the over secretion of dopamine. The result is paranoid schizophrenia; the mania, the upper, the phobia, the splitting of the human personality, and all those elements I taught earlier. On the other hand, there is the undersecretion of dopamine. You may not realize this, but Parkinson's disease is a disease of depression. Parkinson's comes out of depression. Dopamine helps facilitate the control of muscles and the central nervous system, and a Parkinson's case will have the tremors. I believe the reason for Parkinson's is found in Proverbs 13:12, but not just Parkinson's, but other disorders as well. May I show it to you? 'Hope deferred makes the heart sick.'

Hope deferred maketh the heart sick: but *when* the desire cometh, *it is* a tree of life.
Proverbs 13:12

CHOOSING TO OVERCOME DEPRESSION

If you have no hope, you have no faith. If you have hopelessness, you have no faith. Because 'faith is the substance of things hoped for.' Hebrews 11:1 says, "Now faith is the substance of things hoped for."

Now faith is the substance of things hoped for, the evidence of things not seen.   Hebrews 11:1

So if you have hopelessness you are not hoping for anything, thereby you have no faith, and without faith you will have no solutions. Because faith always represents something that should come to pass that has not. About faith, the Word says, "It is the evidence of things not yet seen."

the evidence of things not seen.   Hebrews 11:1b

Faith is the first literal 'tangible intangible' that ever existed. Without faith, it is impossible to please God, because you must come to a place that you operate in a dimension beyond your understanding. At the same time, your understanding is not mystical or superstitious. It is based upon knowledge of God's Word. 'Hope deferred makes the heart sick, but when the desire comes, it is a tree of life.'

Hope deferred maketh the heart sick: but *when* the desire cometh, *it is* a tree of life.
                Proverbs 13:12

Years ago I was in Texas doing a conference, and I met a man that used to be a pastor and his wife, who had brought him. He used to be a pastor, but the deacon board of that church kicked him out after 23 years of service. For the life of me, I do not know who put deacons over the elders, but that is the way it is in many churches in America. It is ungodly order when the deacons rule the elders. The deacons are supposed to assist the elders if I understand the Bible correctly. But they kicked him out, and he developed Parkinson's. Why? Because of hope deferred.

I met him at the end of a Sunday service with his wife. He was there with his tremors, and I heard his story. After listening, I said, "Did God call you to be a pastor or are you a hireling?" He said, "No, I've always wanted to be a pastor and help God's

Chapter 4

people. I became a pastor because I wanted to, not just because I needed a job. I said, "Good answer. If you believe God really called you to pastor the flock and you have been kicked out, you believe your life is over and you have hope deferred which makes the heart sick. Hope deferred results in decreased dopamine levels. Parkinson's is a direct result, biologically, of a reduction in dopamine values. [22] But it says here, 'When the desire comes, it's a tree of life.'"

See, I was trying to ignite this man in faith. I said, "If God called you to take care of the flock then go start another church. Get out of your juniper tree and get over here and go to work." He looked at me and said, "In this condition?" I said, "Sir, you get behind that pulpit and start taking care of the flock. God will send you people, and you minister the gospel and take care of the flock just like this. You preach just like this." His wife was weeping. He was stone cold looking at me.

"You take care of the flock and as the desire comes because you are following your heart, dopamine will be increased, the tremors will go, and God will heal you." Parkinson's is something that can be defeated. I do not know what happened after I left, but I told him the truth because I had the Word to prove it. How about that for a good story?

2 Corinthians 10:4-5 says, "The weapons of our warfare are not carnal, but mighty through God to the pulling down of strongholds."

> **⁴ (For the weapons of our warfare *are* not carnal, but mighty through God to the pulling down of strong holds;) ⁵ Casting down imaginations, and every high thing that exalteth itself against the knowledge of God, and bringing into captivity every thought to the obedience of Christ;**
>
> 2 Corinthians 10:4-5

Section 2
A Different Way of Thinking

I am about to move into another dimension to help you overcome depression. You have to have a different way of thinking. You are going to have to 'flush' the old

---

22. Obeso JA, Rodríguez-Oroz MC, Benitez-Temino B, Blesa FJ, Guridi J, Marin C, Rodriguez M (2008). "Functional organization of the basal ganglia: therapeutic implications for Parkinson's disease". Mov. Disord. 23 (Suppl 3): S548–59. doi:10.1002/mds.22062. PMID 18781672

Choosing to Overcome Depression

personality that has bound you to ungodly thoughts. It is going to take you some time to have your mind renewed. It is going to take you some time to have your spirit energized by the Spirit of God to believe truth again.

Right now, the voice of the enemy and the law of sin is strong. The Word of God and the law of God seem like a soft, small, weak voice. But the more you meditate on God's Word, it will become stronger and stronger and stronger and stronger, and the voice of the enemy will become weaker and weaker and weaker until you make the exchange and take your life back. In the process, your body will begin to serve you. The neurotransmitter imbalances will come back to normal, and you will not have the reinforcement of depression because the foundation for it will be gone and your body will serve you. Freedom with peace of mind is exactly what we are getting in exchange. You can take the word 'incurable' and cast it into the pit. There is no such thing as incurable disease. Do not buy the lie of the Pharisees and the Sadducees. The Sadducees did not believe in the resurrection. They had no hope. That is why they were 'sad, you see.'

Our next scripture from James 1:8 says, "A double-minded man is unstable in all his ways." An adjoining statement from Kings reads, "Why do you halt between two opinions? Let God be true and every man a liar."

> **⁶ But let him ask in faith, nothing wavering. For he that wavereth is like a wave of the sea driven with the wind and tossed. ⁷ For let not that man think that he shall receive any thing of the Lord. ⁸ A double minded man *is* unstable in all his ways.** James 1:6-8

> **And Elijah came unto all the people, and said, How long halt ye between two opinions? if the LORD *be* God, follow him: but if Baal, *then* follow him. And the people answered him not a word.** 1 Kings 18:21

You have to be convinced that God's Word is true. You may say, "Well I'll believe God's Word is true when my symptoms are gone. I'll believe God's Word is true when I'm healed." You will never be healed if that is what you believe. God's Word is true whether you are healed or not healed. That is tempting God. That is trying to

Chapter 4

bribe Him. It is your decision to believe God regardless of your thoughts, feelings or symptoms. If your stability is based on outward signs and wonders, you will be left unstable and unsure of where you stand. While 'a double minded man is unstable in all his ways,' Hebrews 5:14 says, "But strong meat belongs to them that are of full age, even those who by reason of use have their senses exercised to discern both good and evil."

> **But strong meat belongeth to them that are of full age, *even* those who by reason of use have their senses exercised to discern both good and evil.** Hebrews 5:14

There is this vein of thought in the Christian church that if you think about or discuss evil or you use the words 'Satan' or 'evil spirits' you are authenticating them to rule. If you take this perspective, you are going to have to cut out a lot of your Bible that refers to Satan and evil spirits. The Word of God defines what evil looks like including the New Testament. If you have a fear of evil you will avoid those Scriptures. If you have a fear of evil you will pretend they do not exist. Well, evil spirits exist whether you accept or deny the Scriptures about them. In Hebrews, Paul talked to the early church who thought they could handle strong meat and he said, "You're babes; you're such that need to go back on the bottle. For he that is on the milk is unskillful in the word of righteousness.

> **For every one that useth milk *is* unskilful in the word of righteousness: for he is a babe.** Hebrews 5:13

"But he that is of full age is he or she who by reason of use have their senses exercised to discern both good and evil."

> **But strong meat belongeth to them that are of full age, *even* those who by reason of use have their senses exercised to discern both good and evil.** Hebrews 5:14

Folks, 'senses exercised' is a practical application. Practice makes perfect. But we are junkies addicted to a 'quick fix,' and we are so used to taking a pill that we do not realize that 'we are to work out our own salvation daily with fear and trembling.' We do not understand the work part. We want to be fixed with some magical formula or anointed one. But we do not want to go through the effort of changing our spirituality and personality to become changed, even if it may take a few months or years to perfect.

You may say, "Well, that's just too much work." Then stay back there in captivity waiting for some magical formula to remove the requirement that you work out your own salvation. I have to work out my own salvation every day. I have to make up my mind about which law I will follow. I have to cast down many thoughts and feelings in a given day that are not of God. Do you? Because I am tempted does not mean I have sinned. The enemy wants to give you thoughts to tempt you, and you think because you had an evil thought, you have already sinned when it is still temptation. If you believe you have sinned then you will just go ahead and do it. You are too easily deceived.

God wants you to know the difference between what is Him and what is not Him. If you do not know what is of God and what is not of God and if you do not know what is truth and what is error, you will be double-minded in spite of yourself. Without the Word of God, you have no veracity of conclusion. You will be left with supposition, superstition, and other people's voices that you will believe without researching them yourself. You need to study the Word of God for yourself not just believe what you hear on TV, a pulpit on Sunday morning, or audio and video presentations. You need to be a 'workman that needeth not to be ashamed rightly dividing the word of truth' for yourself.

Study to shew thyself approved unto God, a workman that needeth not to be ashamed, rightly dividing the word of truth. 2 Timothy 2:15

But we have become 'Word junkies.' Hebrews 4:12 says, "For the word of God is quick and powerful and sharper than any two-edged sword. Piercing even to the dividing asunder of soul and spirit."

For the word of God *is* quick, and powerful, and sharper than any twoedged sword, piercing even to the dividing asunder of soul and spirit, and of the joints and marrow, and *is* a discerner of the thoughts and intents of the heart. Hebrews 4:12

Chapter 4

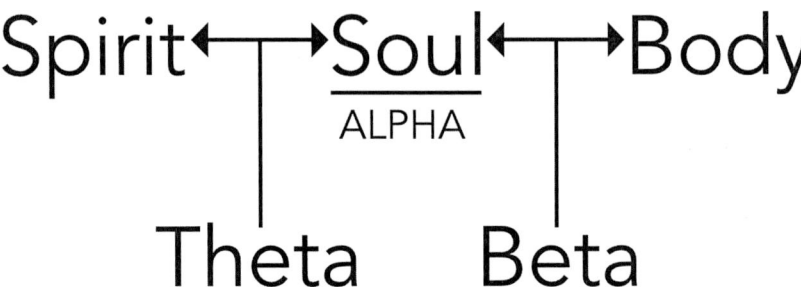

Looking at the Spirit, Soul, and Body chart, you need to address how you interact with God in all three dimensions. Is the Word of God spirit? Yes, because it is a living being; the living Word. For example, at the soul level if you are bound by fear; you are phobic. You think that is just the way you are. You are trembling, phobic, waiting for the bottom to fall out of your life, and have apprehensions. Then I come along with the Word of God, which is spirit, and you are a spirit. So the first place that you ignite with truth is not here where you heard it in your head (mind/soul). Rather it is in your inner man (spirit), where the Holy Spirit is for affirmation and confirmation. Your training and thoughts from the past may interfere with truth, because you have listening to these thoughts over the years. So I come along to disrupt that with a Scripture saying, "God has not given you the spirit of fear, but power, love, and a sound mind."

For God hath not given us the spirit of fear; but of power, and of love, and of a sound mind. 2 Timothy 1:7

However, you may say, "I'm just a fearful person. I've been fearful all my life." I would say to you, "Well, God didn't give you that fear. He didn't give you a spirit of fear so where did it come from?" You may have fear, but you are not fear. Can I call you Fear? Can I change your name to Fear? "Hello, Fear." No, you are not fear. If we could remove fear, then who gets to stay? You do. Would you prefer to be you with fear or without fear? Would you like to be you with bitterness or without bitterness? Would you like to be you with depression or without depression? We can be smart and insightful for others, but we need to apply those insights to our own lives.

So, 'the Word of God is quick and powerful, piercing even to the dividing asunder of soul and spirit.'

> **For the word of God *is* quick, and powerful, and sharper than any twoedged sword, piercing even to the dividing asunder of soul and spirit, and of the joints and marrow, and *is* a discerner of the thoughts and intents of the heart.** Hebrews 4:12

You might be wondering how this is so when you are stuck feeling fearful. The Word of God says, "That fear didn't come from God. You have been given 'power, love, and a sound mind.'" Your mind says, "I'm not very sound." The Holy Spirit says, "Yes, but if we can get rid of fear, then you'll be sound." As you begin to consider the Word of God, it confronts your mindset at the soul level. It divides your thoughts and separates them based upon whether they agree or disagree with the Word. This allows you to have an objective standard of truth and ungodly thoughts are subjected to that truth.

Could I help you solidify this concept? The law of God is superior to the law of sin. So why would you follow 'stinking thinking'? As I said, "The law of God is superior to the law of sin." So if you are going to 'hold every thought captive and you are going to cast down every imagination, every high and lofty thing that would exalt itself against the knowledge of God and bringing into captivity every thought to the obedience of Christ' you have to cast down what is not of God.

Here is how it works. God wants you to know the difference between good and evil. He wants you to grow up, be able to handle strong meat and get off the spiritual baby bottle of milk. You have been around Christianity long enough. We need to rise up and start acting like we are growing up a little bit. But, in your members, you have both the law of God and the law of sin. When the law of sin is still so strong and the law of God is becoming stronger you are going to have to decide that the law of sin is inferior to God's law. Folks, I want to help you because you can defeat every temptation of your life right now. This is an overcoming depression teaching. You can defeat every thought that rules your physiology right now. Your body is ready to respond to chemistry balance, but you will not let it if you are following the law

Chapter 4

of sin, which is inferior. God wants your body to respond to the law of life, which is superior. Do you want your bodies to serve you or do you want to serve your bodies in sickness and disease? Do you want your bodies to serve you? God created your bodies to serve you. You have to help your bodies serve you. How do you do that? By making sure your spirituality and your personality follow more closely the law of God and not the law of sin.

CHAPTER 5:
'GOS-PILLS' FOR YOUR LIFE

For the word of God *is* quick, and powerful, and sharper than any twoedged sword, piercing even to the dividing asunder of soul and spirit, and of the joints and marrow, and *is* a discerner of the thoughts and intents of the heart. Hebrews 4:12

Well, you may say, "I'm too fearful of a person." The Word of God will help you discern that you are not a fearful person, but you have come into agreement with fear. You came into agreement with feelings of hopelessness and despair. You decided to 'major in minors' when it comes to priorities in your life. You have decided to embrace thoughts that are inferior to the Word of God. By your decisions, you have called evil 'good' and refused to call evil 'evil,' because you were comfortable being a survivor rather than a 'thriver.'

Woe unto them that call evil good, and good evil; that put darkness for light, and light for darkness; that put bitter for sweet, and sweet for bitter! Isaiah 5:20

You are not called to be survivors—you are called to be 'thrivers.' The world is full of survivors. You should be a 'thriver.' The world should be depressed. You should be happy, well balanced, and excited sons and daughters of God. You should be excited to be here, on this planet, and get on with the program laid out by the Bible. You may be thinking, "Well, what about others?" I am not talking to others. I am talking to you.

Over the years, I have bumped into keys to depression. These keys are problematic questions stuck in people's minds: who am I, why am I here on this planet, and who cares? I would not be surprised if some of you have struggled with these occasionally. Now I am bringing the issue right down home. Some of the topics

Chapter 5

covered in this teaching may not apply to everyone, but these common questions are a serious problem for humanity. It is a plague even in the Christian church.

Sometimes when people come through for ministry, I ask, "Who are you?" Their reactions make me think they are going to have a heart attack and leave. It is as if I have asked the most horrible question.

They might reply, "Eh, who am I? I don't know. My name is Charlie."

I would reply, "I didn't ask you your name. I said, 'Who are you?' I didn't ask you your name. I want to know who are you on the inside?"

Sometimes in ministry sessions, I pull out a piece of paper and place it in front of them and say, "Write ten things that you believe about who you are on the inside as fast as you can and let none of them be what you do." I want people to reflect on who God made them to be but not based upon their assessment of their accomplishments because who they are is not what they do. However, in today's society, who you are is what you do. According to God, who you are is not what you do. But who you are spiritually, on the inside, is what you will manifest in your actions. In other words, depending on whether you choose to follow God or that other kingdom, it will be reflected in how you think, speak, and act. In turn, this can reflect well or poorly on you. Your value is not based upon your achievements, but what you are manifesting is a good indication of which kingdom you are choosing to follow.

This brings us to the question 'Why am I here?' Some may say, "I know I'm here and I'm just dying to go to heaven one day. As the Bible says, 'It's appointed unto man once to die and then the judgment.' I'm getting ready for that day." Lord, have mercy. Is that why you believe you are here? Some may respond, "Who cares that I'm here?" Addressing these questions are crucial to your ministry right now. I am moving into some sensitive areas here with you. I want you to open your hearts. I appreciated your time and effort reading through this book. I am a very direct teacher. So I know that I have made you gulp a few times and I know it may feel like I am talking to you personally. Even though it may feel uncomfortable to confront certain issues brought up in this teaching, I implore you to deal with them. As I say, "If the shoe fits, wear it." God loves every single one of you, and you are not reading this necessarily because you feel like it. You are reading this because the Spirit of

'GOS-PILLS' FOR YOUR LIFE

God drew you. We are not here to be politicians in Christ and look the part and say all the right things. It is a matter of life or death, folks. You are special, and I love you so much. I wish I had the time to sit down and spend an hour with each of you, just to bond with you and get to know you as my brothers and sisters. It is such a tragedy as a teacher to meet all these special brothers and sisters and not even have the time to hang out with them.

The next question is 'Who am I?' Years ago I had a prophet pull me out of an audience at church when I was young in the Lord, a year and a half as a believer. I will not tell you the whole story, but I remember the words coming out of this prophet's mouth. I did not know him from a cornfield in Iowa, and he did not know me. Through the prophet, God said to me, "You're mine. You belong to me. I've called you to do a work in your generation. Be all that I've called you to be and don't listen to lies." That is all I remember. He went on forever, I do not remember any of it, and I did not get a recording. However, what I heard was enough for me. Those words have burned inside me like a fire for 30 years.

I have no idea what He wanted me to do so I just showed up, and it has evolved over time. I was not called to be an evangelist. I was called to the church to preserve the seed of God in spite of the devil. To bring healing, hope, and deliverance when there seemed to be no hope. I cared when no one else would. You are so special to God and me. Do not ever let anyone tell you that you are not 'the apple of His eye.' Do not let anybody tell you that you are not engraved in the palms of His hands. Do not let anyone ever tell you that your names are not written down in the book of life. Do not let anybody tell you that you are not a son or a daughter of the Father. Let no one tell you that you are not betrothed to the Lord Jesus as a wife. Let no one interfere with who you are. Embrace it, bride of Christ. Embrace it. You may say, "But I'm not ready." He knew that when He saved you. It is amazing that people become born again, and now, after they are saved, they think that God hates them. That is the strangest thing I have ever heard. God saved you, and then you wonder if He even likes you? What is that? That is a crazy thought. Hypothetically, that would mean He saved you because He did not like you. Does that make sense? It is amazing the junk we choose to listen to and believe.

Chapter 5

If you have ever struggled with spirits of heaviness, I want to help you to overcome them, so they will not rule you. You will rule them. In order to do this, I am going to Psalms 139 to read through the whole chapter.

> [1] To the chief Musician, A Psalm of David. O LORD, thou hast searched me, and known *me*.
> [2] Thou knowest my downsitting and mine uprising, thou understandest my thought afar off. [3] Thou compassest my path and my lying down, and art acquainted *with* all my ways. [4] For *there* is not a word in my tongue, *but*, lo, O LORD, thou knowest it altogether. [5] Thou hast beset me behind and before, and laid thine hand upon me. [6] *Such* knowledge *is* too wonderful for me; it is high, I cannot *attain* unto it. [7] Whither shall I go from thy spirit? or whither shall I flee from thy presence? [8] If I ascend up into heaven, thou *art* there: if I make my bed in hell, behold, thou *art there*. [9] *If* I take the wings of the morning, *and* dwell in the uttermost parts of the sea; [10] Even there shall thy hand lead me, and thy right hand shall hold me. [11] If I say, Surely the darkness shall cover me; even the night shall be light about me. [12] Yea, the darkness hideth not from thee; but the night shineth as the day: the darkness and the light are both alike *to thee*. [13] For thou hast possessed my reins: thou hast covered me in my mother's womb.

That word 'reigns' means the inner workings of your existence, the deep recesses of your spirit and who you really are.

> [14] I will praise thee; for I am fearfully *and* wonderfully made: marvellous *are* thy works; and *that* my soul knoweth right well.

I am special. You are special. We need to acknowledge this fact. It is worth saying, "I'm special." Say, "I am fearfully and wonderfully made. I'm special." Wow, this truth is awesome.

> [15] My substance was not hid from thee, when I was made in secret, *and* curiously wrought in the lowest parts of the earth.

That was when you were conceived in the womb of your mother. Even then you were known. Wow.

'GOS-PILLS' FOR YOUR LIFE

> **16 Thine eyes did see my substance, yet being unperfect; and in thy book all *my members* were written, *which* in continuance were fashioned, when *as yet there was* none of them.**

You were planned before your genetic creation was set in motion. You were born of God's mind in creation. You are not an accident. You are a planned event.

Before you were ever conceived God knew you. Before your body parts began to form, when a sperm and egg got together and said, "Hallelujah, praise the Lord! We made it!" Before the process of genetics and biology began in the womb, you were known.

> **17 How precious also are thy thoughts unto me, O God! how great is the sum of them! 18 *If I* should count them, they are more in number than the sand: when I awake, I am still with thee. 19 Surely thou wilt slay the wicked, O God: depart from me therefore, ye bloody men. 20 For they speak against thee wickedly, *and* thine enemies take *thy name* in vain. 21 Do not I hate them, O LORD, that hate thee? and am not I grieved with those that rise up against thee? 22 I hate them with perfect hatred: I count them mine enemies. 23 Search me, O God, and know my heart: try me, and know my thoughts: 24 And see if *there be any* wicked way in me, and lead me in the way everlasting.**
>
> Psalm 139

'Who am I?' There you are in Psalm 139. 'Why am I here?' There you are. 'Who cares?' God cares. Settle it. You are not an accident. You belong. You are a planned event. The devil hates planned events. He is trying to keep you from your birthright by tempting you to listen to lies so he may steal you from God. That is why you need to know who you are and why you are here.

I want to help you to position yourself. I have taught you a variety of subjects, much of which you may forget, but maybe you will get a sense of the bigger picture. There is no possible way you can remember all of what I have taught because of the scope of the subject, but did you get the picture? Is it possible for you to have the ability to take ownership of your life again? Quit listening to lies in your mind. The beginning of freedom begins in Psalm 139 by knowing who you are. Settle it. God is your Father. Settle it that you belong here. No longer will you have 'hope deferred that will make your heart sick.' You must begin to develop the desire to overcome

CHAPTER 5

depression, which is hope and faith. Because 'when desire comes again, it is a tree of life.' The first aspect of life is to love the Lord your God with all of your heart, and your soul, and your mind and love your neighbor as you love yourself.

> **[37] Jesus said unto him, Thou shalt love the Lord thy God with all thy heart, and with all thy soul, and with all thy mind. [38] This is the first and great commandment. [39] And the second *is* like unto it, Thou shalt love thy neighbour as thyself.** Matthew 22:37-39

Folks, this is the beginning of all life. Depression will not allow you to accept yourself, it will not allow you to accept others, and it will not allow you to feel like you are accepted and loved by God. What a lie. I proved that it was a lie by reading Psalm 139. If you ever doubt who you are, go to Psalm 139 until you get it deep inside your heart. Believe it that you may live. You must position yourself in God. God who? The Godhead, comprised of Father God; the Word of God, which is Jesus; and the Holy Spirit. Somebody said the other day, "Well, I'm praying to God." I said, " God who?" They said, "What?" I said, "God who?" They responded, "Does it make a difference?" I said, "Yes. Jesus said it made a difference. Jesus said that in that day we should go to Father God in his name and that we could talk to Father God."

> **And in that day ye shall ask me nothing. Verily, verily, I say unto you, Whatsoever ye shall ask the Father in my name, he will give *it* you.** John 16:23

So are you talking to Father God? Jesus said in that day you should ask him nothing. Are you praying to Jesus? Well, in John 16 Jesus said, "In that day you shall ask me nothing but you shall ask the Father and think not that I shall pray the Father for you. You talk to your Father yourself."

> **[26] At that day ye shall ask in my name: and I say not unto you, that I will pray the Father for you: [27] For the Father himself loveth you, because ye have loved me, and have believed that I came out from God.** John 16:26-27

Read it for yourself in John 16. Is it all there? Get this relationship with the Godhead settled. Quit avoiding the Father of all spirits. Do not be afraid of God. The devil is afraid of God. The devil knows his time is short and he is the father of fear. Why is he so full of fear? He knows his time is short and he wants you to think your time is short. 'He goes about like a roaring lion, seeking whom he may devour, who you are to resist steadfast in the faith.'

> **Be sober, be vigilant; because your adversary the devil, as a roaring lion, walketh about, seeking whom he may devour:** 1 Peter 5:8

Position yourself in the Father, position yourself in the living Word, who is Jesus, and position yourself in the Holy Spirit. They are the source. You have to decide to believe the Word and follow it by applying it in obedience. That way you can position yourself in the Godhead. In John 14:6, Jesus said, "I am the way, the truth, and the life."

> **Jesus saith unto him, I am the way, the truth, and the life: no man cometh unto the Father, but by me.** John 14:6

SECTION 1
YOUR JOURNEY WITH THE WORD

Your life is a journey. You are in the way, but you do not have to be in the way and block your forward progress. Jesus said, "I am the direction you should take. In that direction, remember I am the truth in it. If you find the way you should go and you take me, as the truth in it, then you shall find life. Because I am the way that you should go, I am also the truth in the way, and I am the life as the conclusion of the journey." Psalm 119:105 says, "Thy word is a lamp unto my feet and a light unto my pathway."

> **NUN. Thy word *is* a lamp unto my feet, and a light unto my path.** Psalm 119:105

If I did not know the Word of God, I probably would not be doing well today because all I would have are my own thoughts. Before I was saved years ago, I used to be very afraid. In childhood, I had been victimized and, as a result, if you came

Chapter 5

to the door I would shake like I had palsy. I was so afraid of you that I could never look you in the eyes. I was so afraid. I was so beaten down. I had been verbally, and physically, and emotionally abused as a young man, and I had no confidence left. The Word of God has brought me sanity, and peace, and direction. I love God's Word. God knows more that E.F. Hutton. He loves the neglected people of the world.

Acts 17:28 says, "For in Him we live and move and have our being. As certain also of your poets have said, 'For we also are His offspring (Listen carefully…) For in Him we live, and move and have our being."

> **For in him we live, and move, and have our being; as certain also of your own poets have said, For we are also his offspring.** Acts 17:28

If you 'live, move and have your being' in some other dimension that is not good for you, you are going to have the fruit of something that is bad. You cannot follow the law of sin and have peace and joy. It is not going to happen. Romans 8:14-17: "For as many as are led by the Spirit of God, they are the sons and daughters of God. For we have not received the spirit of bondage again to fear, but we have received the spirit of adoption whereby we cry Abba, Father."

> **[14] For as many as are led by the Spirit of God, they are the sons of God. [15] For ye have not received the spirit of bondage again to fear; but ye have received the Spirit of adoption, whereby we cry, Abba, Father. [16] The Spirit itself beareth witness with our spirit, that we are the children of God: [17] And if children, then heirs; heirs of God, and joint-heirs with Christ; if so be that we suffer with *him*, that we may be also glorified together.** Romans 8:14-17

Settle it. 'If God be for you, who can be against you?' Who cares what people have said and thought about you? It is what He thinks and what He says about you that matters. He, not other people, is the author and finisher of your faith. Get out of idolatry toward people. If you choose to listen to what other people say over what God has said in His Word, you are making them your gods. That is idolatry. Quit being afraid of their voices and their faces. Quit making people your standard. God is the standard of existence.

'GOS-PILLS' FOR YOUR LIFE

The Spirit itself, the Holy Spirit, bears witness with our spirit that we are the children of God.

The Spirit itself beareth witness with our spirit, that we are the children of God:

Romans 8:16

Give yourself a hug. Say, "Wow, I'm a child of God. I escaped like a bird from the snare of the fowler. I escaped from the pollution of my ancestry. I can breathe again. I am a new creature. Behold all things are passed away. Behold all things are becoming new."

Therefore if any man *be* in Christ, *he is* a new creature: old things are passed away; behold, all things are become new. 2 Corinthians 5:17

I like this. It is your journey. It is your faith. If you encounter an evil spirit giving you thoughts say, "Excuse me. I have places to go. Get out of here!" Keep on walking and move forward. 'And when having done all to stand, stand.' Just stand.

Wherefore take unto you the whole armour of God, that ye may be able to withstand in the evil day, and having done all, to stand. Ephesians 6:13

Get a spine. You might say, "Yeah, but everyone might not like me." Remember that is idolatry. God loves you, forget about just 'liking you.' Jesus said, "If you love me, keep my commandments."

If ye love me, keep my commandments. John 14:15

I prefer the term 'love' over 'like.' Father God loves us, and we are His children. 'And if children then heirs; heirs of God, and joint-heirs with Christ.'

And if children, then heirs; heirs of God, and joint-heirs with Christ; if so be that we suffer with *him*, that we may be also glorified together. Romans 8:17

Chapter 5

And be not conformed to this world: but be ye transformed by the renewing of your mind, that ye may prove what *is* that good, and acceptable, and perfect, will of God. Romans 12:2

I hope you are taking note of these scriptures because these are your ministry Scriptures. Here are additional Scriptures for your journey:

Jesus saith unto him, I am the way, the truth, and the life: no man cometh unto the Father, but by me. John 14:6

For in him we live, and move, and have our being; as certain also of your own poets have said, For we are also his offspring. Acts 17:28

[14] For as many as are led by the Spirit of God, they are the sons of God. [15] For ye have not received the spirit of bondage again to fear; but ye have received the Spirit of adoption, whereby we cry, Abba, Father. [16] The Spirit itself beareth witness with our spirit, that we are the children of God: [17] And if children, then heirs; heirs of God, and joint-heirs with Christ; if so be that we suffer with *him*, that we may be also glorified together. Romans 8:14-17

For God hath not given us the spirit of fear; but of power, and of love, and of a sound mind. 2 Timothy 1:7

These are the Scriptures to begin the process of overcoming negative thinking and depression. This is your prescription–your 'gos-pills.' They will defeat depression. Meditate on these Scriptures day and night and embrace them and you might be surprised at the change inside you. Mix it with your faith.

Romans 12:2 says, "And be not conformed to this world, but be ye transformed by the renewing of your mind."

And be not conformed to this world: but be ye transformed by the renewing of your mind, that ye may prove what *is* that good, and acceptable, and perfect, will of God. Romans 12:2

'GOS-PILLS' FOR YOUR LIFE

Why are we going to renew our mind? To replace the law of sin with the law of God. Remember the law of sin has trained you. It is part of your personality. It is part of your persona of existence. It is what draws you down. It has become part of your biology. So it is time to get a new way of thinking. But the Holy Spirit only uses the Word to help you think and reason. For repetition, I said, "The Holy Spirit only uses the Word to help you think." He reminds you of the Word. He brings it back to your remembrance as you learn how to overcome and be an overcomer. 'But be ye transformed by the renewing of your mind that you may prove what is that good and acceptable and perfect will of God' for you.

The next 'gos-pill' is Ephesians 4:23: "And be renewed in the spirit of your mind."

And be renewed in the spirit of your mind; Ephesians 4:23

The next 'gos-pill is Romans 14:8. This takes care of suicidal ideation. This scripture takes care of that deep, dark part of depression. 'For whether we live, we live unto the Lord, and whether we die, we die unto the Lord. Whether we live, therefore, or die, we are the Lord's.' So, what is the big deal with fears and concerns about death?

For whether we live, we live unto the Lord; and whether we die, we die unto the Lord: whether we live therefore, or die, we are the Lord's. Romans 14:8

The next 'gos-pill' is 2 Corinthians 5:6-9.

⁶ Therefore *we are* always confident, knowing that, whilst we are at home in the body, we are absent from the Lord: ⁷ (For we walk by faith, not by sight:) ⁸ We are confident, *I say*, and willing rather to be absent from the body, and to be present with the Lord. ⁹ Wherefore we labour, that, whether present or absent, we may be accepted of him. 2 Corinthians 5:6-9

I went through my 'valley of the shadow of death' a while back. God was with me. I never lost my peace. I never had one second as a downer. I was positive, happy and 'whether I lived or died, I was the Lord's.' But I told God this, "You don't need me up there, Sir, don't let the devil take me out and then give me to you as a gift

Chapter 5

prematurely, because I'm of no earthly good to you in Heaven, Lord. You need me down here, on this planet. I need to be down here to help you with your people. They are hurting. They have no one to tell them the truth that will save their souls. They have made pacts with the enemy, and they call it your will. They're asking servants of Satan to take care of them, and they are charged money for it. I don't want to go home, Father. Let me live, that I may stay here and serve. I got work to do, Lord. I'm too young to go home."

The illness that was trying to kill me had killed every male in my family tree for many generations. Currently, I am the only survivor of generational iniquity in my family tree. I am sure that 'to be absent from the body' would have been nicer since I would be in heaven. However, what are we going do up there? I mean Jesus did not say he needed any help in heaven. He said, "I go away to prepare a place for you if it were not so I would not have told you," and he did not say he needed any help.

In my Father's house are many mansions: if *it were* not *so*, I would have told you. I go to prepare a place for you. John 14:2

Besides, I cannot cut a board straight with a saw. I am a 'wood butcher.' So much for taking care of pearly gates and golden stairs and all the rest. It would be a mess when I got through with it if I was in charge of building places in heaven.

Where we are needed is here on this planet. You have to commit yourself to live your life down here and fulfill the promises of Moses in Psalm 90. 'The longevity of man should be three score and 10 and if by reason of strength four score.' In other words, you should live to about 80+ years old.

The days of our years *are* threescore years and ten; and if by reason of strength *they be* fourscore years, yet *is* their strength labour and sorrow; for it is soon cut off, and we fly away. Psalm 90:10

One of my doctors rebuked me recently. I do not remember exactly what was said. I mentioned something about getting old, and she looked at me and said, "Sir, I'm a doctor, I don't consider people old until they're about 80 to mid-80's. You need to have a reality check. You're just middle-aged, start acting like it." "Oh," I replied.

'GOS-PILLS' FOR YOUR LIFE

I like that doctor. She preached the gospel to me. Quit acting like you are old. As people age, they might say, "Well, I'm just dying to go to Heaven. I'm putting in my time until I pass away." Listen, Moses was 80 before he even started his ministry. He wasted 40 years of his adult life hiding from the Pharaoh in fear. So do not tell me you are too old to start ministering and serving the Lord. Your spirit of man is ageless. So get your body in motion. Get your carcass moving. Do you know what the Bible says? 'The spirit of a man shall sustain him in his infirmity.'

The spirit of a man will sustain his infirmity; but a wounded spirit who can bear?
Proverbs 18:14

A while back, this same doctor said, "I attribute your remarkable recovery from a death disease to three things. The first thing is your incredible belief in God." I did not realize she noticed. I did not say, "I'm a believer in God. I just want you to know that." Nor did I go out of my way to talk about God. She knew who I was and what I do as a pastor, but I did not make a big deal out of it. Why would I boast? She went on to say, "Second, who you are on the inside, a very positive individual and, thirdly, being surrounded by people who love you." Folks, those are the ingredients for life. Loving God, loving myself, and loving others was the way of life that raised me from a death bed. I have to live out the gospel. I have to live what I preach. It was nice. Wow, it works!

The next Scripture is Psalm 30:5. 'Weeping may endure for a night, but joy comes in the morning.'

For his anger *endureth but* a moment; in his favour *is* life: weeping may endure for a night, but joy *cometh* in the morning.
Psalm 30:5

Woo hoo! That is exciting. These are your 'gos-pills.' You can write these scriptures down and use them later. I would write down every one of them and put them on my refrigerator and let them sink in by staring at them whenever I had a chance.

David said, "Restore unto me the joy of your salvation and uphold me with your free spirit, Lord."

Chapter 5

Restore unto me the joy of thy salvation; and uphold me *with thy* free spirit. Psalm 51:12

I have ministered to many people who were down and thought they had committed the unpardonable sin. They were filled with self-loathing and depression along with everything that that entails. I would look at them and say, "Would you repeat after me, please?" and they would respond, "What?" I would say, "Repeat after me. 'Lord.'" They would repeat, "Lord." I would continue, "Restore unto me the joy of your salvation."

They would repeat this statement, and things have happened. I have seen them weep, cry and break when they said, "Lord restore unto me." Because they did not have any joy. Salvation was not a joy; it was a burden of accusation by the enemy. 'Lord restore…' Would you do this for me as you read this? I feel an unction to go in this direction. Out loud say, "Lord restore to me the joy of your salvation." 'The kingdom of God is not meat nor drink, but righteousness, and peace, and joy in the Holy Ghost.' Say, "The kingdom of God is not meat nor drink, but is righteousness, peace, and joy in the Holy Ghost." It may seem odd to say this out loud but it necessary to declare this fact and make this request known.

For the kingdom of God is not meat and drink; but righteousness, and peace, and joy in the Holy Ghost. Romans 14:17

Psalm 126:5-6 say, "They that sow in tears shall reap in joy, he that goes forth and weeps, bearing precious seed, shall doubtless come again with rejoicing, bringing in sheaves of his fruit."

⁵ They that sow in tears shall reap in joy. ⁶ He that goeth forth and weepeth, bearing precious seed, shall doubtless come again with rejoicing, bringing his sheaves with him. Psalm 126:5-6

Nehemiah 8:10-12 describes how the people were in sackcloth and ashes. They were moaning and groaning over the findings of the law. They saw that their ancestors had disobeyed God. Nehemiah said to them, "Stop crying. Go your way, eat the fat, drink the sweet and send portions to them that have nothing that's been prepared, for this day is holy unto the Lord, neither be ye sorry for the joy of the Lord is your strength."

> ⁹ And Nehemiah, which *is* the Tirshatha, and Ezra the priest the scribe, and the Levites that taught the people, said unto all the people, This day *is* holy unto the LORD your God; mourn not, nor weep. For all the people wept, when they heard the words of the law. ¹⁰ Then he said unto them, Go your way, eat the fat, and drink the sweet, and send portions unto them for whom nothing is prepared: for *this* day *is* holy unto our Lord: neither be ye sorry; for the joy of the LORD is your strength.   Nehemiah 8:9-10

I want you to say it, "For the joy of the Lord is my strength. I have a right to be happy. I have a right to be joyful. I have a right to eat, and drink, and make merry, because the joy of the Lord is my strength!"

So the Levites stilled all the people that were crying, weeping, carrying on, saying hold your peace for the day is holy, neither be grieved. All the people went their way to eat, and to drink, and to send portions, and to make great mirth because they had understood the words that were declared unto them.

> ¹¹ So the Levites stilled all the people, saying, Hold your peace, for the day *is* holy; neither be ye grieved. ¹² And all the people went their way to eat, and to drink, and to send portions, and to make great mirth, because they had understood the words that were declared unto them.   Nehemiah 8:11-12

I declare this same statement to you today as you read this. Here is another quote from Isaiah 61:1-4:

> ¹ The Spirit of the Lord GOD *is* upon me; because the LORD hath anointed me to preach good tidings unto the meek; he hath sent me to bind up the brokenhearted, to proclaim liberty to the captives, and the opening of the prison *to them that are* bound; ² To proclaim the acceptable year of the LORD, and the day of vengeance of our God; to comfort all that mourn; ³ To appoint unto them that mourn in Zion, to give unto them beauty for ashes, the oil of joy for mourning, the garment of praise for the spirit of heaviness; that they might

Chapter 5

be called trees of righteousness, the planting of the LORD, that he might be glorified. **⁴ And they shall build the old wastes** (of bipolar inherited diseases. That is included in 'waste.'), **they shall raise up the former desolations, and they shall repair the waste cities, the desolations of many generations.** Isaiah 61:1-4

The gospel allows you to be free of the iniquities of your ancestors if you come out of agreement with what took your parents, grandparents, and great-grandparents into bondage that has been tracking you. These are the things you hate in your parents and grandparents that you end up doing. Your children end up doing them, and your grandchildren end up doing them as well. When are we going to stop this garbage? 'Flush it.' That is how you move forward. When are we going to start making new generations of blessing? Why are we dressing up in the desolation of our ancestors? Why are we carrying their iniquity? You do not have to be a carrier. I do not have to be a carrier of the iniquity of my ancestral line. I am barely escaping it as it is. If I had not understood this and began to allow God to change me, it would have killed me like it killed them. Thank God for truth.

Section 2
Renewing Your Life Like the Eagles

¹ *A Psalm* **of David. Bless the LORD, O my soul: and all that is within me,** *bless* **his holy name. ² Bless the LORD, O my soul, and forget not all his benefits: ³ Who forgiveth all thine iniquities; who healeth all thy diseases; ⁴ Who redeemeth thy life from destruction; who crowneth thee with lovingkindness and tender mercies; ⁵ Who satisfieth thy mouth with good** *things; so that* **thy youth is renewed like the eagle's.** Psalm 103:1-5

I have a story and testimony that exemplifies God's ability to 'renew our youth like the eagles.' A Jewish lady came to me many years ago. She heard about me through a friend who had been healed of some diseases. She came in by phone wanting to know if she could be healed. She wanted to know if she had to accept this 'Jesus' to be healed. I said, "No, you don't have to accept this Jesus to be healed, but if you're healed it will be he and the Father who have done it. What you do with that?

I don't know." She responded, "Well, do I have to be a Christian?" I said, "No, you do not."

She was talking to one of our phone ministers, and he asked her, "What do you have?" She said, "Advanced osteoporosis; I've had it for 30 years. I got it at age 30." She was age 60 when she called us. She had to use a walker to get around. She had no more strength in her bones. She was in trouble. She asked the phone minster, "Well, I hear you guys deal with spiritual roots. What is the root to osteoporosis in my life?"

Her condition was not the result of post-menopausal estrogen deficiency. This was primary osteoporosis. It had been 30 years of affliction. He said to her, " Well the answer to that is in your Jewish scriptures." She said, "What? In our Jewish Scriptures?" As Christians, I hope we know that the Old Testament are the Jewish Scriptures. Come on now, work with me, Christians. The entire Old Testament are Jewish scriptures, did you know that? Sometimes Jewish people do not know the Torah, and the Writings, and the Prophets anymore than Christians know their Bible either. She said, "In the Jewish scriptures? What does it say in the Jewish scriptures?" Now, we had her attention. "Well, it says in Proverbs 14:30 that 'envy and jealousy is the rottenness of the bones.'"

A sound heart *is* the life of the flesh: but envy the rottenness of the bones. Proverbs 14:30

Envy and Jealousy are behind osteoporosis because it is a 'rotting of the bones.' The minister proceeded to ask, "Did you ever have any problem with envy and jealousy?" She said, "Yes, all through childhood. Everybody was prettier than me. All of them had better boyfriends and better jobs. I've always had envy and jealousy. How would you know that?"

Our phone minister replied, "Because you have the disease coming out of it." He said to her, "What do you think you need to do about this?" She said, "Well, I think I need to call this sin and repent to God." Honestly, I wish I could get Christians to think that fast sometimes. She knew it. She was busted.

He said, "Okay, are you ready to repent to God for envy and jealousy and ask the God of Abraham, Isaac, and Jacob to forgive you?" "Yes," she said. She did it from her

Chapter 5

heart. Thirty days later she went to her doctor for her annual checkup. She walked into his office without her walker. She walked under her own power. They took their tests, and a couple of weeks later she went in for the results. Her doctor said to her, "All evidence of osteoporosis has been halted in your body. We're showing a bone density increase of 15-18% structure wide. What have you been doing?"

Her reply, "Repenting to the God of Abraham, Isaac, and Jacob for envy and jealousy." They do not have that insight in medical school. They do not even have that in psychiatric schools. He said to her, "You have the bones of a 30-year-old women, and we don't understand." When she repented to the God of Abraham, Isaac and Jacob God restored her bones to the year that her bones were taken by the villain. The latter part of Psalm 103:5 happened to this Jewish lady. "Who satisfies your mouth with good things so that your youth is renewed like the eagles." Her youth was renewed like the eagles. Fly, baby, fly. Fly, baby, fly.

Who satisfieth thy mouth with good *things; so that* thy youth is renewed like the eagle's.

Psalm 103:5

I just came back with a doctor's report about my life. The doctor said, "Well, it's amazing we don't really see any evidence of this issue being a problem in your life anymore. In fact," my doctor continued, "as to what we see there is no reason why you cannot live out a long, productive life." I was told this a couple of months ago. As of this writing, I am 74. I did not want to go to heaven too fast. God is good all the time. The promise of Moses in Psalm 90 is this: "If by reason of strength four score." Thank you, Lord, for the strength for the next ten to twenty years. We have got work to do in Jesus' name. I want to finish this teaching with you embracing the Scriptures, and then I want to pray for you as the conclusion.

Isaiah 35 is one of the most powerful chapters in the whole Bible. In fact, if you have been around Be In Health® teachings, it is known as the seventh 'R of freedom.' The '8Rs to Freedom' represent eight concepts related to the process of overcoming sin in our life. In order, they are known as Recognize, take Responsibility, Repent, Renounce, Remove, Resist, Rejoice and Restore. The one we are discussing happens to be the seventh. It is called Rejoice. In this case, it means to give God thanks. God

'Gos-pills' for Your Life

is good, and His mercy endures forever unless we cancel it through disobedience. Unless we cancel it through ignorance or 'yeah, but…' Just let my words minster to your heart. Let this be your song of rejoicing. Add this to the list of scriptures I have given you as the 'gos-pills' for overcoming depression. It will assist you in your struggle with depression and your relationship with others. Let this be an incredible statement for your life.

The following scriptures from Isaiah chapter 35 represent your journey out of depression.

> [1] The wilderness and the solitary place shall be glad for them; and the desert shall rejoice, and blossom as the rose. [2] It shall blossom abundantly, and rejoice even with joy and singing: the glory of Lebanon shall be given unto it, the excellency of Carmel and Sharon, they shall see the glory of the LORD, *and* the excellency of our God. [3] Strengthen ye the weak hands, and confirm the feeble knees. [4] Say to them *that are* of a fearful heart, Be strong, fear not: behold, your God will come *with* vengeance, even God *with* a recompence; he will come and save you. [5] Then the eyes of the blind shall be opened, and the ears of the deaf shall be unstopped. [6] Then shall the lame *man* leap as an hart, and the tongue of the dumb sing: for in the wilderness shall waters break out, and streams in the desert. [7] And the parched ground shall become a pool, and the thirsty land springs of water: in the habitation of dragons, where each lay, *shall be* grass with reeds and rushes. [8] And an highway shall be there, and a way, and it shall be called The way of holiness; the unclean shall not pass over it; but it *shall be* for those: the wayfaring men, though fools, shall not err *therein*. [9] No lion shall be there, nor *any* ravenous beast shall go up thereon, it shall not be found there; but the redeemed shall walk *there*: [10] And the ransomed of the LORD shall return, and come to Zion with songs and everlasting joy upon their heads: they shall obtain joy and gladness, and sorrow and sighing shall flee away.   Isaiah 35

Section 3
Concluding Prayer

As we conclude this teaching, I want to pray for you. While I may have never met you, the following prayer represents my heart and desire for you as you continue your journey out of depression:

Chapter 5

Father God, these are Your promises, the highway of holiness. Even though we may have been wayfaring fools, we were smart enough to wake up and apprehend Your promises. The highway of holiness is the narrow gate. There be few that find it. And the wide gate is a wide road to destruction, and many will find it.

Father, deal with us as sons and daughters. Rebuke the devour for their sake. Father, I pray that even though the 'god of this world' has blinded their minds to the simplicity of the gospel of love that You, Father, by Your Spirit would strip away the blindness from their minds and their spirits. Let them apprehend the joy of their salvation. They are going to put off spirits of heaviness and put on the garment of praise. They are going to step out of their prison houses of darkness, and they are going to look around and say, "This is my planet; the earth and the fullness thereof is the Lords. It is our planet. Thank you, Father, for saving me to be a part of it."

Father, I pray that You would teach them to discern evil spirits in operation in their life so they may overcome that other kingdom and its mindset. Help them to discern spirits of heaviness and confusion operating in their life. Help them to recognize double-mindedness, rejection, bitterness, shame, guilt, and fear. Help them to identify the enemy's traps with Your help. These spirits are no longer in darkness. They are being exposed to light. Now, they recognize that other kingdom. Lord, send the 'Finger of God' against the enemy not only so You will defeat that kingdom, but that they will defeat the enemy for themselves in Your name and in Your power. Father, give them strength to overcome.

Let them begin to see who they really are. Precious, precious, precious sons and daughters. Precious, goofy sons and daughters. But You love goofy sons and daughters. You saved me, as a son, and I was goofy. Father, let the words that I have written penetrate deeply to divide the spirit from the soul. Father, let the words that I have written, by Your Spirit, cause things to come to their remembrance that they may recover themselves from the snare of the devil. Give them the power to overcome. Give them discernment. Let their eyes be opened. Let them see so that darkness and light will be the same unto them. That in the darkness it is as if it were light. That the darkness will not hinder their journey because You have let the gospel be the light that is a lamp unto our feet and a light unto our pathway. In our darkest night, we may see our journey, and see where we are going, and shrug the rest off, and keep on moving. Let us be overcomers.

Father, I pray that they begin the process of having their mind renewed by the 'washing of the water of the Word.' Let them begin to enact the law of God in their members that they may have an antidote to the law of sin in their thoughts. Let them know that they are fearfully and wonderfully made and the hand of God is upon them. They are not junk. They are brands that are plucked from the fire of hell. They are brands that are plucked from the fire of death and destruction. 'And He looked down, and He had favor on them for surely his mercy endureth forever.'

Father, soften our hearts. Give us tender hearts towards You again. Let us repent to You, Father, for our ungodly fear and dread of You. We may have associated You with an earthly father that may not have loved us. Father, let us begin the process of loving ourselves. Remind us when the enemy would come and begin to accuse us that we would say, "In Jesus name, shut up, you're a liar."

Let us begin the process of holding every thought captive, casting down every imagination. Thoughts such as: 'Who told you were naked?' 'Who told you, you were full of shame?' 'Who told you, you were full of fear?' 'Who told you, you were full of guilt?' 'Who told you, you are no good and God does not love you?' Those thoughts were not from You. So, we let You, Father God, be true and every man a liar. Perish the thought. 'Flush it.'

Father, I bless these people, I do not curse them. Father, I bless them with all spiritual blessings in Heavenly places. Father, I ask You, by Your Spirit, that You will go with them, overshadow them, not just for their lives, but for their children, and their children's children's lives. That they will become oracles and vessels of light and salt, oracles for the destruction of darkness and the establishment of Your love for mankind through them. Establish them as recovering, wounded servants helping others be healed. We are all wounded and pierced servants helping others recover. Father, I give these people to You in Jesus name. Amen. God bless you.

BIBLIOGRAPHY:

1. American Psychiatric Association (2013), Diagnostic and Statistical Manual of Mental Disorders (5th ed.), Arlington: American Psychiatric Publishing, pp. 160–161, ISBN 978-0-89042-555-8, retrieved 1 MAY 2017

2. Diagnostic and Statistical Manual of Mental Disorders, Fifth Edition (DSM-5). American Psychiatric Association. 2013

3. Christine Heim; D. Jeffrey Newport; Tanja Mletzko; Andrew H. Miller; Charles B. Nemeroff (July 2008). "The link between childhood trauma and depression: Insights from HPA axis studies in humans". Psychoneuroendocrinology. 33 (6): 693–710. doi:10.1016/j.psyneuen.2008.03.008. PMID 18602762. Retrieved 24 April 2017

4. Gabbard, Glen O. Treatment of Psychiatric Disorders. 2 (3rd ed.). Washington, DC: American Psychiatric Publishing. p. 1296

5. Yang, Qing. "Gain Weight by "going Diet?" Artificial Sweeteners and the Neurobiology of Sugar Cravings: Neuroscience 2010." The Yale Journal of Biology and Medicine. YJBM, June 2010. Web. 24 Apr. 2017

6. Walton, R. G., R. Hudak, and R. J. Green-Waite. "Adverse Reactions to Aspartame: Double-blind Challenge in Patients from a Vulnerable Population." Biological Psychiatry. U.S. National Library of Medicine, July 1993. Web. 24 Apr. 2017

7. "Depressive Disorders." Psychology Today. Sussex Publishers, 27 Dec. 2015. Web. 24 Apr. 2017

8. Brookmeyer, R., and S. Gray. "Methods for Projecting the Incidence and Prevalence of Chronic Diseases in Aging Populations: Application to Alzheimer's Disease." Statistics in Medicine. U.S. National Library of Medicine, n.d. Web. 24 Apr. 2017

9. I. Ashok, Dapkupar Wankhar, Wankupar Wankhar, and R. Sheeladevi. "Neurobehavioral Changes and Activation of Neurodegenerative Apoptosis on Long-term Consumption of Aspartame in the Rat Brain." Journal of Nutrition & Intermediary Metabolism 2.3-4 (2015): 76-85. Web. 24 Apr. 2017

10. Moore, AB Thomas J. "Demographic Differences in Adult Use of Psychiatric Drugs." JAMA Internal Medicine. American Medical Association, 01 Feb. 2017. Web. 24 Apr. 2017

11. "Diagnostic Evaluation and Treatment." Northwest Behavioral Medicine. N.p., n.d. Web. 24 Apr. 2017

12. Clark MS, Jansen K, Bresnahan M (November 2013). "Clinical inquiry: How do antidepressants affect sexual function?". J Fam Pract. 62 (11): 660–1. PMID 24288712

13. Molero, Yasmina, Paul Lichtenstein, Johan Zetterqvist, Clara Hellner Gumpert, and Seena Fazel. "Selective Serotonin Reuptake Inhibitors and Violent Crime: A Cohort Study." PLOS Medicine. Public Library of Science, 15 Sept. 2015. Web. 24 Apr. 2017

14. Kluger, Jeffrey. "Is Drug-Company Money Tainting Medical Education?" Time. Time Inc., 06 Mar. 2009. Web. 24 Apr. 2017

15. Wilson, Duff. "Harvard Medical School in Ethics Quandary." The New York Times. The New York Times, 02 Mar. 2009. Web. 24 Apr. 2017

16. Anderson IM, Haddad PM, Scott J (Dec 27, 2012). "Bipolar disorder". BMJ (Clinical research ed.). 345: e8508. doi:10.1136/bmj.e8508. PMID 23271744

17. Christie KA, Burke JD Jr, Regier DA, Rae DS, Boyd JH, Locke BZ: Epidemiologic evidence for early onset of mental disorders and higher risk of drug abuse in young adults. Am J Psychiatry 1988; 145:971–975

18. Sham, P. C., C. J. MacLean, and K. S. Kendler. "A Typological Model of Schizophrenia Based on Age at Onset, Sex and Familial Morbidity." Acta Psychiatrica Scandinavica. U.S. National Library of Medicine, Feb. 1994. Web. 24 Apr. 2017

19. Kendler KS, Karkowski LM, Walsh D (1998) The structure of psychosis. Arch Gen Psychiatry 55:492–499

20. Terao, Takeshi, and Teruaki Tanaka. "Antidepressant-induced Mania or Hypomania in DSM-5." SpringerLink. Springer Berlin Heidelberg, 19 Nov. 2013. Web. 24 Apr. 2017

21. Eguale, Tewodros, David L. Buckeridge, Aman Verma, Nancy E. Winslade, Andrea Benedetti, James A. Hanley, and Robyn Tamblyn. "Association of Off-label Drug Use and Adverse Drug Events in an Adult Population." JAMA Internal Medicine 176.1 (2016): 55. Web

22. Obeso JA, Rodríguez-Oroz MC, Benitez-Temino B, Blesa FJ, Guridi J, Marin C, Rodriguez M (2008). "Functional organization of the basal ganglia: therapeutic implications for Parkinson's disease". Mov. Disord. 23 (Suppl 3): S548–59. doi:10.1002/mds.22062. PMID 18781672